The Art of

Listening

to Young People

Amoris Christi

En Route Books and Media, LLC
Saint Louis, MO

⊕*ENROUTE*
Make the time

En Route Books and Media, LLC

5705 Rhodes Avenue

St. Louis, MO 63109

Contact us at **contact@enroutebooksandmedia.com**

Cover Credit: Amoris Christi

ISBN-13: 979-8-88870-087-7

Library of Congress Control Number: 2023945470

To you, Mary, to whom the generations have confidently turned, assured that you always listen. Under your mercy, *Theotokos*, this book is dedicated to you.

TABLE OF CONTENTS

FOREWORD

A long time ago when I was a young priest, my bishop once shared with me the secret to leadership: listening! He explained that if people do not feel heard and have a chance to voice their concerns, ideas, or beliefs, then I would never be able to truly help them and lead them. Through the years, this wisdom has proven true; indeed, leadership is listening!

If we are to accompany and assist our young people along the journey of life, then we must listen to them. *The Art of Listening to Young People* offers just such tools to help those of us who work with the young church to hear their concerns and love them in the present moment. This book is a fascinating read and offers insight into the minds and hearts of our young people. If we are to listen, we must be in relationship with the person; relationship leads to receptivity as we empathically listen to the person in front of us.

The young person speaking to us is not a problem to be solved, but a person to love and respect by attentively listening to their thoughts and concerns. That certainly does not mean that we cannot respond or offer direction in their lives, but unless they feel heard, our advice will fall on deaf ears. This correlates to another one of my life's realizations that we must chose "people over projects." It takes patience and grace to stop, be present, and actively listen to another when there are seemingly many other things "to do." This book reminds the reader to ask for patience and grace to listen attentively to the person before us.

Having just returned from World Youth Day in Lisbon, Portugal with Pope Francis and 1.3 million young people, I was reminded once again of the art of accompaniment and listening. In fact, that is the whole point of the Holy Father's invitation for us to be a more synodal church – we cannot "journey with" another person without listening to their hearts. My prayer is that this short book will offer tools to help us be better listeners so that we may truly lead our youth closer to Christ and His Church.

For anyone who wants to be a better listener, especially to our youth, I highly recommend this book.

Bishop David L. Toups, SThD
Diocese of Beaumont
August 15, 2023
The Solemnity of the Assumption of the Blessed Virgin Mary

INTRODUCTION

How do we communicate with today's young people? How do we get our message across to them? When questions such as these plague the minds of many of us who labor in the Church, it may seem odd to write a book about *listening* to young people. Part of the confusion comes from a wrong understanding of listening, which is sometimes viewed as a kind of permissiveness or relativistic coddling. We, on the other hand, believe that listening is *transformative*. It is an active and intentional form of *accompaniment* and *ministry*, which is mutually edifying. A popular quote says, "Preach the gospel at all times; when necessary, use words." Listening is preaching the Gospel with only a few words. Like other forms of witnessing, it also opens the door of credibility that precedes giving guidance and teaching. Listening is first of all a way of encountering the mystery of another person with reverence and love. When done well, it is one of the purest forms of *being with* another person.

Before we go further, we must know to whom we are referring when we talk about listening to *young people*. The term "youth" is after all fraught with ambiguity. "Youth" in the United States refers to teenagers, and "young adults" refers to people older than 18 and up to around 25 years old. In other countries, the definitions can be substantially different. The largest consensus on this question comes from the United Nations. Beginning in the mid-1960s, the Member States decided to bring greater focus to youth participation, development, and peace. Eventually, 1985 was proposed as an International Youth Year, and "youth" was defined as comprising those between the ages of 15 and 24.[1] But since "youth" means something different in the United States, we have opted to call this group *young people* instead. Most people do not take these ages rigidly, and neither do we. UNESCO, for example, makes this explicit when it writes, "As the experience of being young can vary substantially across the world, between countries and regions, we consider 'youth' as a flexible category."[2]

Youth

For statistical purposes, the united nations defines 'youth' as persons aged between 15-24. However, this definition is not universal. As the experience of being young can vary substantially across the world, between countries and regions, we consider 'youth' as a flexible category. As such, context is always an important guide in UNESCO's definition of youth.

The book that you are about to read, *The Art of Listening to Young People*, was written by a small team of researchers and clinicians from different fields, who also have years of first-hand experience ministering to young people. This book is therefore an unusual combination of pastoral application and scientific grounding,

---

[1] UN Secretary General, "International Youth Year: Participation, Development, Peace," Report of the Secretary General (United Nations, June 1981), https://digitallibrary.un.org/record/21539/files/A_36_215-EN.pdf.

[2] "Youth | UNESCO," accessed July 19, 2023, https://www.unesco.org/en/youth.

meant primarily for those who accompany young people in one-on-one settings like mentoring, formation, spiritual direction, or counseling. It hopes to be inspirational, but it does not shy away from being technical, citing some of the most fascinating research across a variety of disciplines. We know that drawing inferences for pastoral application from highly specialized research or experiments poses the risk of confirmation bias. Suffice it to say, we have done our best to bridge both worlds and to extrapolate the most helpful and practical guidance for those who accompany young people. To further assist in application and assimilation, each chapter is concluded with a summary of its key points and a few questions for self-reflection.

As you read this book, we hope that you become as convinced as we are that listening to young people is the need of our times. We hope that you will join us in striving to become better listeners through continued learning, practice, and self-reflection. Most importantly, we hope this book inspires you to reach out to the young people around you more meaningfully through the art of listening.

CHAPTER 1

The Ministry of Listening

Listen

['lisn] verb

To hear something with thoughtful attention.
"evidently he was not listening". "if I've had a long day I love to listen to music and chill.

*Merriam-Webster Dictionary

Before you read this chapter, take a minute to listen. There are sounds all around you. You *hear* them all, but you *listen* only when you intentionally focus on some sounds that you hear. You can listen to the sound of someone typing nearby or birds chirping outside. If you do, notice how your attention shifts. At the outset, let us say that this book is not about hearing young people but about listening to them. It is about listening to that young person that you are accompanying, so that you may accompany them well. Whenever we listen with the tender heart of Christ, we affirm people's dignity, we heal wounds, and we deepen relationships. We also expand our understanding and break free from any narrow-mindedness. In the subsequent chapters, we will look at the possibilities and challenges of listening to young people. Drawing from faith and science alike, we will identify the skills that we need to cultivate and the negative habits that we need to let go of. But first, let us start more broadly with acknowledging the breadth and power of listening, which is quite simply one of the most impactful ministries that we can exercise for young people today.

Why listen to young people?

The idea of 'listening to young people' can raise eyebrows. Somewhere in the semantic range of the word *listen*, there is a hint of implying *obedience* or *docility*.[1] At the very least, you have to give your attention to the other, which means suspending your own thoughts and speech. At Mount

Tabor, while the three disciples were in a frenzy at the sight of Jesus with Elijah and Moses, the "voice from the cloud" announced, "This is My beloved Son; *listen* to Him!" (Matt 17:5). Indeed, the word ἀκούετε (a-koo-ete) also means "obey."[2]

So, this is the underlying issue: who should be speaking, and who should be listening? From time immemorial, the order has been set. The teacher speaks, and the disciples listen. In communities or families, elders

---

[1] Andrew D. Wolvin, *Listening* (Madison: Brown & Benchmark, 1996), 30–31.

[2] Timothy A. Gabrielson, "Obedience," in *Lexham Theological Wordbook*, ed. Douglas Mangum and others, Lexham Bible Reference Series (Bellingham, WA: Lexham Press, 2014).

speak, and youngsters listen. In the social hierarchy, such as in a corporation, those at the lower rung of the ladder must listen to those who are higher up. Reversing this order can be upsetting. After all, wisdom comes through experience, and young people have the least experience. Someone might say, "Why should we listen to today's young people? Their generation has serious issues. They should be listening to us!" To be clear, listening in this book's context has nothing to do with authority, obedience, or social hierarchy. Listening is about receiving. It is welcoming the other, in recognition of their personhood, and making space in one's heart for the reality of another person's unique existence and story. As the next chapter explains, listening is a form of love, and love has the power to heal and transform.

Listening to a troublesome student

One of our authors explains his experience of listening to a student, whom we will call Victor, who caused serious trouble at his college.

Many years ago, the college in India where I worked as a professor endured severe unrest. Political factions had an undue influence upon some of our students and resulted in violent demonstrations on campus. The students who were involved were dismissed pending inquiry, while two of us were designated as inquiry officers. Our detailed report resulted in disciplinary measures being taken against thirteen students. In time, especially as we involved their parents or guardians in the process, the students understood their mistake and resolved to do better – all except one.

Victor was a second-year undergraduate student. In class, he was pleasant and well-behaved, but the investigation revealed that he was the mastermind behind the violent incidents on campus. The case became more complicated when we received complaints from other colleges about his behavior as well. The dorm where he resided filed a complaint relating to sexual abuse, and there was a complaint about his involvement in a brawl in the city square. Enough was enough! Stern action was in the offing.

The next step was to have a series of meetings. When Victor was asked to bring in his parents, he insisted that his father not be informed or invited, though, with further insistence, he eventually obliged. We first met with his family together, then with his parents and him separately. The meetings were difficult, as can be imagined, by the very nature of the topic. For me personally, though, the real challenge had to do with an internal conflict. The administration had entrusted me with finding a solution that would protect the institution. I therefore looked at Victor through an institutional lens: he was a disciplinary problem. The incident was a threat to the college's discipline, safety, and order. Victor was a problem that needed solving, and I was called upon to solve it. All this being the case, something in my heart called me to question my attitude. Was Victor just a problem for me to solve? I gradually recognized that I had to look at Victor as a person first and not as a problem. I needed to connect with him, with his life, his thoughts, and his struggles. In short, I needed to *listen* to him. I therefore determined that I would first try to listen to him and journey with him rather than just quash his rebellion by force.

The next challenge was getting past my web of prejudices. Among fellow professors and colleagues, we held general impressions about "the youngsters these days" that were not helpful. These general biases, together with the specific ways that Victor dressed, the language he used, the reports of his past activities, and the recent incidents, coalesced into what seemed like a clear picture of "his type." I knew in my heart that to serve this man well and ultimately to serve the college well, I had to break free from these prejudices and the resultant mistrust and resentment. I had to genuinely try to understand him. Leaving my stance of rigidity and judgment, I opted for a disposition of compassion and understanding. Before meeting with him, I reminded myself of who I wanted to be, saying to myself, "Don't react in anger. Don't try to intimidate him. See the good in him. There must be a reason why he acted this way. I love this young man. I want to understand him. Let me listen to what he has to say."

I did this much to prepare myself as a listener. But of course, none of this means that Victor would trust me. I was in a position of authority, and he would ultimately be at the receiving end of our disciplinary measures. I reflected on this disparity of power and hoped to make it as easy as possible for him to trust me. Fortunately, building rapport was easier than I thought. I sensed that Victor, from past experience, was expecting an insensitive and adamant officer of institutional policy. My manners and words must have thrown him off balance in a positive way. Thanks to the internal preparation I did beforehand, my facial expression, body posture, and general demeanor were kind and friendly at our first meeting with him and his parents, even as I spoke honestly and frankly. "As you know, the college has tasked me with a detailed inquiry to arrive at suitable disciplinary steps. But I want to do more than that. Significant challenges and crises arise in every person's life. When properly utilized, these dark moments can become new beginnings. On the one hand, the situation may call for disciplinary measures, but I would also like to work together towards a constructive outcome." This approach worked well. Some of the defensive walls came down surprisingly quickly, and the family began to open up. We began to take a fresh look at all that had transpired.

Earlier, Victor and his mother had told me privately that Victor's father was excessively harsh and would not be amenable to reason. The sequence was always the same. Victor would act out mischievously, and his mother would protect him from harsh punishment by concealing it from her husband. Over the years, the father had become essentially clueless about his own son. Today was different, though. He listened to everything. And when he became aware of all his son's actions, he did not explode in wrath. He simply broke down. His tear-streaked face was hardly a believable sight for his wife and son. At that moment, Victor's father terribly regretted his lack of involvement in the life of his family.

In my private sessions with Victor, he reflected on and analyzed each aspect of his life and actions. Here and there, I prompted him with a question, sometimes directing his focus on a particular aspect of his life or asking him to provide me with details he missed. Of course, I tried not to be too intrusive or inquisitive, often reminding him that he could refrain from telling me any details he did not wish to discuss. But surprisingly, Victor was eager to come out with his thoughts, yearnings, and fears. Perhaps, he never had the chance before. As he let it all out, he gradually understood why he was acting out. He was now experiencing a whole new level of self-awareness.

On my part, I prepared a narrative of the events and the young man's part in the unfortunate developments on campus. When the college read my report, they naturally concluded that Victor could not continue there. But by the time our many hours of conversations were finished, Victor himself understood the gravity of his actions and that he could not continue there. He became convinced that he needed a new start in life and that he would find it elsewhere. It was a pleasant surprise that Victor and his parents actually welcomed this decision wholeheartedly.

For a while, I kept in touch with Victor. If he had not broken free from his repeating pattern of misbehavior, his story would have been just one tragedy after another. Instead, being listened to was a pivotal moment for him. They say that all is well that ends well. Well, Victor joined a new program at another institution, where he made good use of his time and his second chance. He landed a job abroad, and I was even fortunate enough to meet him once during my travels. I found him happily settled there and living a good life. Deep within, I thanked the Lord for changing my heart and giving me the grace and wisdom to genuinely listen to him all those years ago.

"The Apostolate of the Ear"

As Victor's story exemplifies, when you take the time to listen to a young person, amazing things can happen. Pope Francis explains, "The most important task in pastoral activity is the 'apostolate of the ear' – to listen before speaking, as the Apostle James exhorts: 'Let every man be quick to hear, slow to speak' (1:19). Freely giving some of our own time to listen to people is the first act of charity."[3] Below, we list some significant outcomes that can result from listening to a young person.

Benefits Of Listening

Improved understanding and relationships: Just think of parents and their teenage children. Perhaps this is the archetypal example of the total inability to understand one another. Often enough, the misunderstandings multiply over the years, and both parties end up speaking at each other, as though in two different languages. Meanwhile, the strained relationship somehow fledges along, with parents resorting to threats and children finding solace in subterfuge. What would happen if parents took the time to genuinely listen? Again, listening does not mean obeying, nor is it merely hearing. Listening goes beyond the surface of wants and demands and strives to understand the heart, to understand the inner turmoil or searching from which all kinds of behaviors emerge. Listening paves the way for genuine mutual understanding. Traditional wisdom, also captured in Stephen Covey's *The 7 Habits of Highly Effective People*, says "Seek first to understand, then to be understood." Taking the initiative to listen and understand builds relationships. And relationships lead to better mutual understanding.

Guidance and support: Once a relationship is developed, once a young person feels understood, they often seek out guidance and support. Youth is a time of many difficult decisions that have long-lasting, even life-long, impact. When they know that they are being listened to, it is a short step for them to soon ask for guidance. They will ask you for examples from your own life. "How did you discern your vocation?" They will approach you for answers. "How do I deal with distractions in prayer?" Listening leads to guidance, but guidance should never move forward without continued listening. As guides, we know only too well that our story is far from perfect and that we are still searching for answers to many of the same questions. Therefore, we guide with a posture of listening – listening to the young person and listening to what the Holy Spirit is doing in the heart of the young person.

Finding and amplifying their voice: Youth is a time of fresh perspectives and creative ideas that are highly innovative but easily neglected by society. Due to their age, socioeconomic position, or inexperience, teenagers and young adults are not often taken seriously by adults. Young people often struggle to articulate their aspirations in a presentable way. Their ideas might not incorporate all factors and considerations because of their lack of experience. As listeners, we can help young people find their voice, giving them the confidence to enter wholeheartedly into the dialog that shapes the present and future of civilization.

Socialization: Humans are created for social living. That is why it is nearly impossible to hold children back from their playmates. This does not always continue as children grow older. During adolescence, social dynamics, such as peer pressure and in-group exclusivity, emerge with greater complexity and intensity. In this journey of socialization, a person needs the support of parents and older mentors to learn conflict-resolution and healthy social participation. In clubs and youth empowerment programs, facilitators are essential in helping young persons integrate with the group and fulfill their specific roles and responsibilities. Listening plays a singular role here. A timid young person may find it challenging to speak up in the group; someone else in the group may express their emotions strongly, and others easily get hurt by it; someone from a different cultural background may feel discriminated against; or gradually, a section of members could become troubled and identify as an anarchic subgroup. These challenges may be found in any social group, whether that be a campus ministry, a corporation, a parish, or a seminary. When adults listen to their struggles and provide an anchoring presence, young people can continue building healthy relationships and maturing in social participation.

Crisis management: Sometimes young people will have to face a very challenging situation, such as a physical, emotional, relational, academic/professional, or faith-related crisis. In the face of life's tragedies, there is no single answer that makes everything better. Some events will even cause a life-altering upheaval. Others will dampen a person's enthusiasm and joy. When suffering comes, listening is the truest form of *being-with*. Whether as a counselor, spiritual director, parent, mentor, or friend, listening is a special way of reflecting the nearness of Christ, who comes close to us in our sufferings and trials.

The loneliness epidemic

In May 2023, Dr. Vivek Murthy, the U.S. Surgeon General, released an 81-page report raising the alarm about the devastating impact of the country's epidemic of loneliness and isolation. He explained how he undertook a cross-country 'listening tour' when he heard stories from many Americans that surprised him. They felt isolated, invisible, and insignificant, making him realize that social disconnection was far more common than he had realized. Loneliness poses an unprecedented threat to everyday living. He writes,

> *Loneliness is far more than just a bad feeling—it harms both individual and societal health. It is associated with a greater risk of cardiovascular disease, dementia, stroke, depression, anxiety, and premature death. The mortality impact of being socially disconnected is similar to that caused by smoking up to 15 cigarettes a day, and even greater than that associated with obesity and physical inactivity. And the harmful consequences of a society that lacks social*

connection can be felt in our schools, workplaces, and civic organi-
zations, where performance, productivity, and engagement are di-
minished. [4]

Loneliness levels are the highest among the elderly (above 70) and young adults (below 30).[5] Sadly, the rate of young adults' loneliness has *increased every year* between 1976 and 2019.[6]

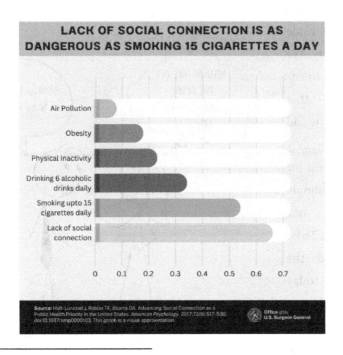

<hr />

[4] Vivek Murthy, "Our Epidemic of Loneliness and Isolation: The U.S. Surgeon General's Advisory on the Healing Effects of Social Connection and Community," May 2, 2023, https://www.hhs.gov/sites/default/files/surgeon-general-social-connection-advisory.pdf.

[5] Louise C. Hawkley et al., "Loneliness from Young Adulthood to Old Age: Explaining Age Differences in Loneliness," *International Journal of Behavioral Development* 46, no. 1 (January 1, 2022): 39–49, https://doi.org/10.1177/016502542-0971048.

[6] Murthy, "Our Epidemic of Loneliness and Isolation: The U.S. Surgeon General's Advisory on the Healing Effects of Social Connection and Community," 19.

The call to better listening

The world is desperately searching for genuine, interpersonal encounters and relationships. More profoundly, the world is a broken heart searching for the love of God. Whenever we listen to another person with sincerity and attention, we reflect to them some ray of that love which has been revealed to us in Christ Jesus. In listening, we may have to hold back our preconceptions, preferences, and preformed judgments, for Christ even put aside his divinity. We may have to enter into that person's world to truly understand them, for Christ willingly assumed our humanity. To be Christ to the world of today is to be open and ready for such genuine encounters in love and truth.

Almost everyone thinks they listen well!

Let listening, attentive and heartfelt listening, be our response to the growing sense of isolation in our society. So many take listening for granted and are seldom intentional about it. In fact, *almost everyone* thinks they listen well, even when most do not.[7] Meanwhile, our inadequate ways of listening lead to alienation and hurt and so many lost opportunities of building trust.[8] If we desire it and are willing to work on it, with God's grace, we can surely become better listeners. We can learn to be present to young people and cultivate healing relationships. We can be Christ to the world. Listening to young people is the way forward. It is the remedy for our isolated world. *Listening is the powerful ministry to young people that Christ is calling us to today.*

Key Points:

1. Listening with an open mind and heart gives young people dignity, heals wounds, deepens relationships, expands understanding, and breaks us free from narrow-mindedness.

2. Listening does not mean obeying. It means receiving the other and making space in one's heart for their unique existence and story.

3. Listening builds relationships with young people, creates a foundation for offering guidance and support, helps them find their voice, assists in their socialization, and helps them in times of crisis.

4. Loneliness is an epidemic that has particularly affected young people today. Christ calls us to cultivate healing relationships by witnessing his love through listening.

---

[7] Clay Drinko, "We're Worse at Listening Than We Realize," *Psychology Today* (August 4, 2021), https://www.psychologytoday.com/us/blog/play-your-way-sane/202108/were-worse-listening-we-realize.

[8] Dan Bobinski, "The Price of Poor Listening," Management-Issues.com, (February 3, 2016), https://www.management-issues.com/opinion/6564/the-price-of-poor-listening/.

Reflection Questions:

1. As you read this chapter, in what ways have you felt inspired to listen better to young people?

2. The story of Victor emphasizes the transformative power of listening. Have you ever experienced a situation where active listening played a crucial role in resolving a conflict or guiding someone towards positive change? How did listening contribute to the outcome?

3. When have you felt less alone just because someone listened to you? Have you ever felt isolated because there was no one to listen to and understand what you were going through?

CHAPTER 2

Because He First Listened to Us

In his book *Life Together,* Dietrich Bonhoeffer wrote, "Just as love to God begins with listening to His Word, so the beginning of love for the brethren is learning to listen to them. <u>It is God's love for us that He not only gives us His Word but also lends His ear.</u> So it is His work we do for our brother when we learn to listen to them."[1] Bonhoeffer recognized that there is an intrinsic connection between love and listening. We are made capable of giving love because we have first received God's love. In an analogous way, we can only give of ourselves as listeners because God has first listened to us. Only when you know what it is like to be listened to, to be understood and known, can you extend the same to the young people around you. 1 John 4:19 says, "We love because he first loved us." With the

intrinsic connection between love and listening in mind, we can derive a similar principle: *We listen because he first listened to us.*

God is himself the communion of three divine persons who, being perfectly united, give and receive totally in love. God therefore created man from

---

[1] Dietrich Bonhoeffer, *Life Together: The Classic Exploration of Christian in Community,* 1st edition (HarperOne, 1978), 97.

communion and for communion. "Then God said, 'Let us make man in our image, after our likeness… So God created man in his own image, in the image of God he created him; male and female he created them" (Gen 1:26-27). It is in man's very nature to mirror the communion of the Trinitarian persons, to receive and to be received, indeed, to listen and to be listened to. The second creation account of Genesis conveys a relationship where God and man speak and listen to each other. God asks Adam a question, "Where are you?", and then listens to his response. He goes on to similarly ask Eve about the matter, listens to her response, and then communicates the consequences (Gen 1:9-16). Though this conversation occurs in the context of the Fall, the text presents divine-human conversation as a preexisting and ordinary part of their relationship.

Throughout the Old Testament, the Lord called man back into relationship with him by the covenants he made through the patriarchs and prophets. These covenants did not just represent man's obligation towards the Lord but also the Lord's attentiveness to man's plight. When the Lord promises Abram a great reward, we see Abram freely expressing his sadness about having no heir. "O Lord God, what will you give me, for I continue childless…?" (Gen 15:2). The Lord listens and promises him a countless multitude of descendants. Chief among the prophets was Moses, who enjoyed an astonishing closeness with God: "Thus the Lord used to speak to Moses face to face, as a man speaks to his friend" (Ex 33:11). Although the Lord gave Moses the commandments and spoke much to Him, He also listened to Moses, such as when Moses vented angrily saying, "Why have you dealt ill with your servant?... Did I conceive all this people? … I am not able to carry all this people alone; the burden is too heavy for me. If you will treat me like this, kill me at once…" (Num 11:11-15). Indeed, the Lord listened to Moses and responded by instituting seventy elders over Israel. The book of Deuteronomy ends with the words, "And there has not arisen a prophet since in Israel like Moses, whom the Lord knew face to face..." (Deut 34:10), which conveys to us that, far from condemning Moses for conversing freely with God, the Lord was pleased to listen and be in conversation with him. In many similar ways throughout the Old Testament, the Lord God revealed himself not as one who merely speaks and commands but as one immersed in dialogue with us, listening and responding with love.

The psalms are prayers welling from the urgent longing of the human heart to be heard: "I say to the Lord, You are my God; give ear to the voice of my pleas for mercy, O Lord!" (Ps 140:6). The psalms often beg the Lord not to be deaf to our cry (Ps 28:1) and then celebrate the fact that God hears us. "I love the Lord, because he has heard  my voice and my supplications. Because he inclined his ear to me, therefore I will call on him as long as I live" (Ps 116:1-2). We can identify easily with the psalmist who cries out from need or despair and then finds consolation in being listened to by God. Even before we receive the answer we are crying out for, just knowing that God knows – that he truly *listens* – is a consolation and relief. "You have kept count of my tossings; put my tears in your bottle. Are they not in your book?" (Ps 56:8). Indeed, the Lord hears the cry of the poor (Ps 34:6).

The relationship between God and man, imperfectly realized in the Old Covenant, culminates in the marriage covenant between God and Man through Jesus Christ. Jesus is "the mediator of a new covenant," (Heb 12:24) who establishes it through his blood. When the author of the letter to the Hebrews described Christ's coming into the world, he beautifully interpreted the following words of Psalm 40 as part of a conversation between the Son and the Father. Christ says, "Sacrifices and offerings you have not desired, but *a body* you have prepared for me" (Heb 10:5). The Letter to the Hebrews was written in Greek. Therefore the author, as he quotes Psalm 40:6, referenced a popular Greek translation of the Old Testament called the Septuagint. But there was a peculiar difference between the versions of Psalm 40:6 found in the Hebrew Old Testament and in the Septuagint. For some reason the Hebrew word "my ears" (אָזְנַיִם) ended up becoming the Greek word "body" (σῶμα). Through mysterious workings of the Holy Spirit, a few hundred years before Christ (when the Septuagint was being written), "you have opened my ears" in Psalm 40:6 became "a body you have prepared for me."[2] The original Hebrew "you have opened my ears" signified that the Lord gave his chosen one *total receptivity* to the will of God. The later Greek "a body you have prepared for me" signified that the Lord gave his chosen one a *body*. Which one is true? Clearly, both are true and they explain each other when understood in the context of the Incarnate Son of God. *Jesus is the open ear to the Father*. He came into the world (assumed a body) to *listen* to the Father and to do his will in everything. He lives on the Father's word like we live on ordinary food (Mt 4:4, Jn 4:34). And the Father for his part *always listens* to the Son. Jesus reveals as much when he prays, "Father, I thank you for hearing me. I

---

[2] For various theories on how or why this may have happened, see Craig R. Koester, *Hebrews: A New Translation with Introduction and Commentary*, vol. 36, Anchor Yale Bible (New Haven; London: Yale University Press, 2008), 433.

know that you always hear me…" (Jn 11:41c-42a). Their boundless, mutual listening is nothing but the expression of their perfect, Trinitarian love.

In Jesus, we are taken up into this wonderful mystery of mutual listening, and we have certainty that our prayers are heard by the Father. He tells his disciples, "In that day you will ask nothing of me. Truly, truly, I say to you, whatever you ask of the Father in my name, he will give it to you" (Jn 16:23). Our hearts are consoled because God truly listens to us, because we are known and understood by him. By his grace, we are now called to extend the same to the young people around us. *We listen because he first listened to us.* Dietrich Bonhoeffer went on to write, "He who can no longer listen to his brother will soon be no longer listening to God either…This is the beginning of the death of the spiritual life."[3] Since we aim to be spiritually alive, to be filled with love of God and neighbor, let us generously give ourselves to listening attentively to the young people that the Lord has placed in our lives.

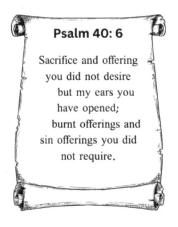

Psalm 40: 6

Sacrifice and offering
you did not desire
but my ears you
have opened;
burnt offerings and
sin offerings you did
not require.

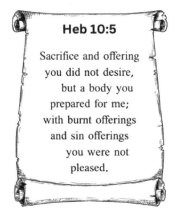

Heb 10:5

Sacrifice and offering
you did not desire,
but a body you
prepared for me;
with burnt offerings
and sin offerings
you were not
pleased.

---

[3] Bonhoeffer, *Life Together*, 98.

Key Points:

1. Love and listening are intrinsically connected. Just as love for God begins with listening to His Word, love for others begins with learning to listen to them.
2. Man is created in the image of God, who exists as a communion of the Father, Son, and Holy Spirit. Reflecting this communion, humans are designed to receive and be received, to listen and be listened to.
3. Throughout the Old Testament, God listens to man. His attentive listening is demonstrated through His interactions with figures like Moses. The Psalms express the human longing to be heard by God and the comfort of knowing that He listens.
4. Jesus is an open ear to the Father, and the Father, in turn, always listens to the Son. Through Jesus, believers are invited into the mystery of mutual listening, where they listen to the Father and they are confident that the Father listens to their prayers. Being listened to by God engenders the ministry of listening to young people.

Reflection Questions:

1. How does your experience of having felt listened to by God help you listen to young people?
2. Why does God listen to us? Why should we listen to young people?
3. How does being permeable to God's word and to the thoughts and feelings of others make you more Christ-like?
4. How is the call to love others fulfilled through listening?

CHAPTER 3

The Context of Young People Today

To listen well to young people, we must do our best to understand their context. New generations create new worlds that, while they overlap with those of prior generations, have distinct characteristics and values. Before we go into specific listening types, behaviors, and practices in subsequent chapters, let us take a closer look at the young people today to whom we are called by Christ to listen.

According to Pew Research, the Millennial generation comprises those born between 1981 and 1996. Beginning with those born in 1997, we have a new generation called Generation Z (or "Gen Z").[1] As of 2023, Gen Z includes anyone roughly between thirteen and twenty-six years old. (In effect, this book could have been called *The Art of Listening to Gen Zs*.[2]) We want to try to grasp their worldview, the way they think, and what they care about, all so that we can listen to them more effectively. They have perspectives, habits, priorities, and beliefs different from prior generations, though in many respects similar to those of Millennials. While always appreciating the uniqueness of each individual, we want to

---

[1] Michael Dimock, "Defining Generations: Where Millennials End and Generation Z Begins," *Pew Research Center* (blog), January 17, 2019, https://www.pewresearch.org/short-reads/2019/01/17/where-millennials-end-and-generation-z-begins/.

[2] As mentioned in the Introduction, this book defines "young people" according to the UN definition of "youth" as those between the ages of 15 and 24. See UN Secretary General, "International Youth Year: Participation, Development, Peace," Report of the Secretary General (United Nations, June 1981), {https://digitallibrary.un.org/record/21539/files/A_36_215-EN.pdf}.

identify some of their most common characteristics. The topic of under-standing Gen Zs, like most generational research, is incredibly complex and fraught with contradictory viewpoints.[3] These viewpoints can be highly subjective and anecdotal. They can also be idealistic, as writers project their hopes for a brighter tomorrow. They are the academic equivalent of popular sentiments for or against "the young people these days." By contrast, this chapter only attends to a few well-substantiated characteristics that are relevant to listening. These are backed by massive, quantitative surveys that capture how young people think or by expert consensus. Once each characteristic is identified, it is interpreted for its potential bearing on the ministry of listening.

Some Key Characteristics of Gen-Z

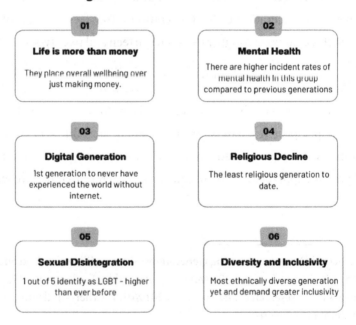

01

Life is more than money

They place overall wellbeing over just making money.

02

Mental Health

There are higher incident rates of mental health in this group compared to previous generations

03

Digital Generation

1st generation to never have experienced the world without internet.

04

Religious Decline

The least religious generation to date.

05

Sexual Disintegration

1 out of 5 identify as LGBT - higher than ever before

06

Diversity and Inclusivity

Most ethnically diverse generation yet and demand greater inclusivity

---

[3] Jennifer J. Deal, David G. Altman, and Steven G. Rogelberg, "Millennials at Work: What We Know and What We Need to Do (If Anything)," *Journal of Business and Psychology* 25, no. 2 (June 1, 2010): 191–99, https://doi.org/10.1007/s10869-010-9177-2.

Life is more than money

According to a large and diverse study of 22,000 young people in 44 countries conducted by Deloitte (2022), the top two reasons among both Millennials and Gen Zs for choosing their current place of work does not include money.[4] The two most common reasons are work/life balance and learning and development opportunities, with finance being only the third most common. Forty percent of them plan to leave their current employment within two years, and one out of three say they would leave their job even if they did not have another opportunity lined up. When it comes to work and life priorities, they clearly have higher values than financial success. They make choices for things like quality of life, relationships, and mental health, and they are unwilling to sacrifice these for financial security or prosperity. Broadly speaking, we might say, they care about *life* more than money. Almost 4 out of 10 Gen Zs have at some point turned down a job that conflicted with their personal ethics. More than half look into the environmental impact and policies of a company before deciding to join it. In listening to today's young people, we must be attentive to their noble aspirations for a meaningful life because their desires extend beyond the traditional trajectory of career-success that older generations might be used to.

Oddly enough, the same survey shows that "my long-term financial future" is the most common cause for stress for both generations. Even though they stand ready to leave their current jobs, they fear financial insecurity. In fact, they are more risk-averse and fear-driven than prior gen-

---

[4] Deloitte, "The Deloitte Global 2022 Gen Z and Millennial Survey | Deloitte Global," May 14, 2023, https://www.deloitte.com/global/en/issues/work/genz-millennialsurvey.html.

erations, in part because their childhood was shaped by the global financial crisis called the Great Recession.[5] So, they do worry about money, but their actual choices appear to be determined by a more wholesome understanding of life. In some ways, they are caught between the ideal of meaningfulness and the fear of financial insecurity. Sometimes, this dilemma causes a young person to become stuck or "freeze." Other times, they pursue wealth but feel unsatisfied with life as they do so.

Their desire for meaningful work connects well with the Christian notion of vocation. In his letter to young people, *Christus Vivit*, Pope Francis writes, "Your own personal vocation does not consist only in the work you do, though that is an expression of it. Your vocation is something more: it is a path guiding your many efforts and actions towards service to others... it is a recognition of why I was made, why I am here on earth, and what the Lord's plan is for my life."[6] Today's young people appreciate this sense of a vocation that transcends the pursuit of money. If we listen well to their hearts, we can help them discover their upward calling in Christ (Phil 3:14) and their capacity to transform the world. By listening to their hopes and dreams, we can draw out their noblest aspirations and give them confidence to pursue them. At the same time, they may need to grow accustomed to the perseverance and patience required to be able to fashion a meaningful ideal from the commonplace matters of daily life and work.

---

[5] Michael Maloni, Mark S. Hiatt, and Stacy Campbell, "Understanding the Work Values of Gen Z Business Students," *The International Journal of Management Education* 17, no. 3 (November 1, 2019): 100320, https://doi.org/10.1016/j.ijme.2019.100320.

[6] Francis, "Christus Vivit," March 25, 2019, paras. 255–256, http://www.vatican.va/content/francesco/en/apost_exhortations/documents/papa-francesco_esortazione-ap_20190325_christus-vivit.html.

Mental health woes: needing encouragement, not protection

In trying to understand Gen Z, one cannot ignore the preponderance of mental health challenges. "More than 9 in 10 Gen Z adults (91%) said they have experienced at least one physical or emotional symptom because of stress, such as feeling depressed or sad (58%) or lacking interest, motivation or energy (55%)."[7] The last fifteen years or so have been a nightmare for mental health. The percentage of American high school students experiencing persistent feelings of sadness or hopefulness *increased 40%* between 2009 and 2019.[8] Between 2007 and 2018, suicide rates among youth ages 10-24 in the US *increased 57.4%*.[9] Compared to prior generations, young people today report higher rates of anxiety, depression, and distress and have the least positive outlook on life.[10,11]

---

[7] Sophie Bethune, "Gen Z More Likely to Report Mental Health Concerns," *Monitor on Psychology* 50, no. 1 (January 2019), https://apa.org/monitor/2019/01/gen-z.

[8] Center for Disease Control and Prevention, "Youth Risk Behavior Survey Data Summary & Trends Report: 2009-2019" (Center for Disease Control and Prevention, 2019), https://www.cdc.gov/healthyyouth/data/yrbs/pdf/YRBSData-SummaryTrendsReport2019-508.pdf.

[9] Sally C. Curtin, "State Suicide Rates among Adolescents and Young Adults Aged 10–24 : United States, 2000–2018," ed. National Center for Health Statistics (U.S.). Division of Vital Statistics., National vital statistics reports ; v. 69, no. 11, 69, no. 11 (September 11, 2020), https://stacks.cdc.gov/view/cdc/93667.

[10] Erica Coe et al., "Addressing Gen Z Mental Health Challenges | McKinsey," Mckinsey, January 14, 2022, https://www.mckinsey.com/industries/healthcare/our-insights/addressing-the-unprecedented-behavioral-health-challenges-facing-generation-z.

[11] The higher rates of mental health challenges among Gen Zs could be *partially* caused by the increased awareness and reduced stigma about seeking psychological help. However, there are many other factors that suggest an overall increase in psychological problems, such as the aforementioned statistics from

The Surgeon General, Dr. Vivek Murthy, issued an unusual public health advisory called "Protecting Youth Mental Health" in December 2021. His report indicates that scientists who have attempted to identify the cause of this decline in youth mental health have come back with a variety of reasons, such as, "the growing use of digital media, increasing academic pressure, limited access to mental health care, health risk behaviors such as alcohol and drug use, and broader stressors such as the 2008 financial crisis, rising income inequality, racism, gun violence, and climate change."[12] Suffice it to say, the causes are likely complex and difficult to ascertain definitively. Here, we focus on understanding young people's mental health from the perspective of how we can help them through listening. Our hope is that, as we lovingly listen to them, we will help them seek God's grace and navigate through all the aforementioned risk factors to emerge stronger.

One reason for the increased anxiety is likely the excessive concern for safety (including by "helicopter parents") and the resulting lack of resilience found in children. This becomes a vicious cycle when the conditioned fragility of children then invites even greater protectionism from adults.[13] This problem began with Millenials, who were raised with much higher parental involvement and feedback than prior generations.[14] As a result, we have "Young people, 18 years and older, going to college still

---

the CDC or the increasing number of school shootings and violent outbursts of mobs in universities, for example.

[12] Vivek Murthy, "Protecting Youth Mental Health The U.S. Surgeon General's Advisory," 2021, 8, https://www.ncbi.nlm.nih.gov/books/NBK575984/pdf/Bookshelf_NBK575984.pdf.

[13] Greg Lukianoff and Jonathan Haidt, *The Coddling of the American Mind: How Good Intentions and Bad Ideas Are Setting Up a Generation for Failure* (New York: Penguin Books, 2018), 29–30.

[14] Maloni, Hiatt, and Campbell, "Understanding the Work Values of Gen Z Business Students."

unable or unwilling to take responsibility for themselves, still feeling that if a problem arises they need an adult to solve it."[15] Incredibly, the problem has become so severe that some young people in America today find ordinary tasks to be overwhelming, including taking an Uber alone or being outside without their phone.[16] In these trivial examples, it becomes painfully clear that being "overwhelmed" by such experiences would not be a good enough reason to be protected from them. On the contrary, it is only by *facing* these situations that they would be able to grow in the maturity and resilience necessary for survival and success.

Empathically listening to young people is powerful and healing, as we know from the success of counseling and spiritual direction. However, the listener should be careful not to "coddle" the young person, exacerbating their anxiety by reacting in tandem, or perpetuating the harmful pattern of protectionism.[17] As we listen, our intent must be to simply remain with them in the struggle and to provide encouragement for them to face it. We must forgo the satisfaction of swooping in and saving them like parents and countless other adults have done throughout their lives. By refraining from doing so, we communicate a deep trust in their capacity to rely upon God, to overcome adversity, and to grow through it. One of the principles of Carl Rogers' person-oriented therapy is that when people are provided with an empathic environment, their own inner drive to self-

---

[15] Peter Gray, "Declining Student Resilience: A Serious Problem for Colleges," *Psychology Today*, September 22, 2015, https://www.psychologytoday.com/us/blog/freedom-learn/201509/declining-student-resilience-serious-problem-colleges.

[16] Korby, Holly, "Young Adults Are Struggling with Their Mental Health. Is More Childhood Independence the Answer?," KQED, December 20, 2022, https://www.kqed.org/mindshift/60624/young-adults-are-struggling-with-their-mental-health-is-more-childhood-independence-the-answer.

[17] See Chapter 7 for more details on the harmful patterns of enabling and codependency through listening.

actualize will direct them forward. His approach is also called client-directed therapy because it is the client who leads rather than the therapist. We must let the young person lead when it comes to the project of their own existence. True listening must aid the young person to become self-standing rather than psychologically or spiritually dependent upon the pastoral minister. The primary value of listening is *presence* or *being-with*, in imitation of Christ who is *God-with-us*. Listening provides a space within which young people can come alive in the recognition of their own agency and begin to see themselves as the protagonist of their own story.

News Events Stressing Gen Z

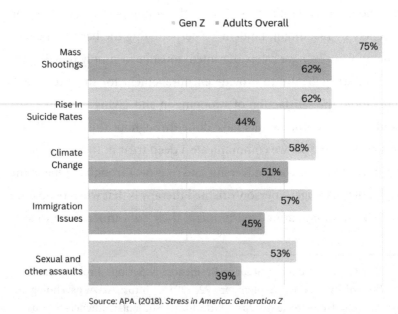

Source: APA. (2018). *Stress in America: Generation Z*

The digital generation

Gen Z is the first generation to have never experienced a world without the internet. What might seem constraining and unnatural to older generations is perfectly normal and effortless for them. This is of course always the case with new technologies throughout history. Older people might find it difficult to communicate over text message because tone and other nonverbal cues are absent, for example. However, young people have found ways around this limitation, using a wide array of emojis and gifs, as well as imbuing the subtle variations of spelling, punctuation, symbols, and capitalization with emotional signification. For this reason, just as people can easily detect the accent of a non-native speaker, Gen Zs and Millennials can detect the writing style of someone who is not fluent in digital communication because of its being plain, formal, and uninflected.

> Should the communication be okay, ok, K, kk, k, or something else? To a postmillennial, these five responses have come to communicate drastically different messages. A response of k. means "you're in big trouble" for two reasons related to perceived intentionality. First, the letter is lowercase, indicating that the sender took the time to "undo" the capitalization that would have automatically occurred (given that the phone capitalizes the first letter of a text), and second, there is a period (full stop) after the letter. If a sender took the extra time to "personalize" the response in this way, it must mean that they were not happy.[18]

Because of their fluency in digital communication, Gen Zs experience near-perfect continuity between textual, audio, video, and in-person social interactions. To listen to them, we must be willing to enter into their world, to encounter them in the avenues in which they communicate and express themselves. We believe that insisting upon only listening in ways with which we are comfortable would not be sufficiently evangelistic or

---

[18] Roberta Katz et al., *Gen Z, Explained: The Art of Living in a Digital Age* (Chicago, IL: University of Chicago Press, 2022), 16.

pastoral. 73.7% of millennials and Gen Zs in the US communicate more digitally than in-person and a similar number would rather text than call, if they had to choose one.[19] Contrary to stereotypes, however, they also greatly value in-person communication. The difference is that they see all these forms of communication as mutually complementary and as part of one seamless continuum.

"Why can't he just follow us on Instagram like everyone else?"

Gen Zs use social media as a creative way to express themselves. They put much thought into choosing what they post for the world and their friends to see. This can of course be taxing, especially if they are trying to construct a social media personality that is liked by many and wins many followers. Teens have mixed opinions about social media, with almost an equal split between some saying it is helpful and some saying it can be a place of bullying.[20] The 2023 Surgeon General's advisory titled "Social Media and Youth Mental Health" observed that researchers have identified both positive and negative effects of social media and that there is still a need to understand its effects better. At the same time, some of the negative effects on adolescents are truly alarming.

---

[19] Rurick Bradbury, "The Digital Lives of Millenials and Gen Z," 3,11, https://liveperson.docsend.com/view/tm8j45m.

[20] Monica Anderson, "Teens, Social Media and Technology 2018," *Pew Research Center: Internet, Science & Tech* (blog), May 31, 2018, https://www.pewresearch.org/internet/2018/05/31/teens-social-media-technology-2018/.

A longitudinal cohort study of U.S. adolescents aged 12–15 (n=6,595) that adjusted for baseline mental health status found that adolescents who spent more than 3 hours per day on social media faced double the risk of experiencing poor mental health outcomes including symptoms of depression and anxiety. As of 2021, 8th and 10th graders now spend an average of 3.5 hours per day on social media... a study conducted among 14-year-olds (n = 10,904) found that greater social media use predicted poor sleep, online harassment, poor body image, low self-esteem, and higher depressive symptom scores with a larger association for girls than boys.[21]

Gen Zs post less on social media compared to Millennials, which could be related to their risk-aversion. On the other hand, communicating their thoughts or preferences in a world that cancels or publicly shames people can be genuinely anxiety-provoking. Another reason for less posting could be that Gen Zs get tired of having to capture the attention of their peers by always writing something "relevant" on platforms where there are so many people simultaneously competing for attention.[22] They seem to prefer passively scrolling through social media instead.[23] Listening to young people today means providing them with a space where they can securely and comfortably reveal themselves without the pressure of

---

[21] Office of the Surgeon General, "Social Media and Youth Mental Health — Current Priorities of the U.S. Surgeon General," June 21, 2023, 6–7, https://www.hhs.gov/surgeongeneral/priorities/youth-mental-health/social-media/index.html.

[22] Katz et al., *Gen Z, Explained*, 24.

[23] Erica Coe et al., "Gen Z Mental Health: The Impact of Tech and Social Media | McKinsey," Mckinsey Health Institute, May 20, 2023, https://www.mckinsey.com/mhi/our-insights/gen-z-mental-health-the-impact-of-tech-and-social-media.

having to be "interesting" or "likable" to keep people's attention and without the fear of being canceled or shamed. They should know that they have our undivided attention because they are unique and wonderful masterpieces of God. They should sense our genuine interest and awe about who they are, just as they are. These meaningful, human interactions will provide young people with an authentically social space where they can truly be themselves. This would stand in contrast to the exaggerated and unbalanced social dynamics of social media platforms that feed into comparison tendencies, often resulting in anxiety and lower self-esteem.[24]

Caught in the religious decline

Over the past three decades, religious faith has continued to decline in America, so that Gen Z is the least religious generation of all. The percentage of Americans unaffiliated with any religion has steadily increased as follows:[25]

The Silent Generation	9%
Baby Boomers	18%
Generation X	25%
Millennial	29%
Generation Z	34%

---

[24] Mary Sherlock and Danielle L. Wagstaff, "Exploring the Relationship between Frequency of Instagram Use, Exposure to Idealized Images, and Psychological Well-Being in Women," *Psychology of Popular Media Culture* 8, no. 4 (2019): 482–90, https://doi.org/10.1037/ppm0000182.

[25] "Generation Z and the Future of Faith in America," *The Survey Center on American Life* (blog), 2022, https://www.americansurveycenter.org/research/generation-z-future-of-faith/.

This trend extends into Catholicism as well. Of course, quantitative data can only tell us so much. It never tells us the whole story, and we might rightly ask further questions. While previous generations have a higher percentage of Catholics, how many of these are Catholic solely because they were born into it? How many are true disciples of Christ? We also know that today countless young people are finding Christ and giving their lives to him in extraordinary ways. Still, the data does tell us that presupposing people's religious affinity or adherence is no longer possible. When working with young disciples of Christ, we should not become frustrated as we listen to their many questions, moral struggles, and difficulties with points of Catholic faith. In many ways, these young people are the heroes of this generation who simply need our encouragement. By listening to them and understanding their challenges, we can witness the gentle power of Christ who does not hesitate to embrace all our frailty even as he calls us to greater holiness.

Sexual disintegration

The percentage of Americans who identify as LGBT doubled to 7.2% between 2012 and 2022.[26] Out of this 7.2%, over half identify as bisexual, one out of five identify as gay, one out of seven identify as lesbian, and one out of ten identify as transgender. Only about one in a thousand Americans identify as queer, pansexual, or asexual. While these numbers look relatively tame, the figures specifically for Gen Zs are startling. Nearly *one out of five of all Gen Z adults identify as LGBT*. This is 1.75 times more than Millenials and six times more than Generation X. Two-thirds of this

---

[26] Gallup Inc., "U.S. LGBT Identification Steady at 7.2%," Gallup.com (Feb. 22, 2023), https://news.gallup.com/poll/470708/lgbt-identification-steady.aspx.

group identify as bisexual. As Christians and pastoral ministers, we cannot simply close our eyes and ears to these realities or write them off as the problem of a small, rogue segment of society. The problem is ubiquitous and the accompaniment of young people today inevitably involves listening to their struggles and the lack of meaningful direction in the area of sexual integration, healing, and maturation.

Sexuality is at the very core of our humanity. When we think of what these young people are going through, our hearts ought to be moved with compassion. Teens who identify as lesbian, gay, or bisexual are approximately *four times* as likely to have made a suicide plan or to have attempted suicide in the last year.[27] This is in addition to the already alarming levels of mental health problems mentioned above. In other words, our young people are hurting. We are called to listen to them with empathy and understanding, not with condemnation. If we stand in rigid judgment, masking and compensating for our own unintegrated sexuality and shame, we will only lead them further astray. Instead, when we are actively receptive to divine love, so that it heals and transfigures our affectivity and sexuality, our very presence will become healing. As loved and healed persons, we will be able to listen to young people like Christ and as Christ. We will be able to acknowledge their longings for love and meaning, intermingled with brokenness and pain, and point to Christ as the true fulfillment of all desire.

---

[27] Center for Disease Control and Prevention, "Youth Risk Behavior Survey Data Summary & Trends Report: 2009-2019," 99–100.

Diversity and inclusivity

Gen Z is the most ethnically diverse generation yet.[28] Gen Zs were raised in this highly interconnected world where information from anywhere is instantaneously accessible. Unlike people in traditional societies, Gen Zs grew up being exposed to diverse cultures and perspectives thanks to the internet and social media. As a result, they find it easier than previous generations to interact with people who look, speak, or act differently than they do. They utilize social media platforms and online activism to raise awareness, challenge systemic biases, and mobilize for change. They demand greater inclusivity in movies, TV shows, advertisements, and other forms of media. According to a recent study conducted by Monster, 83% of Gen Zs consider an employer's commitment to diversity and inclusion as a crucial factor when deciding where to work.[29] In another poll, it was found that 75% of Gen Z respondents would reconsider applying to a company if they were dissatisfied with its diversity and inclusion efforts.[30]

This movement towards diversity and inclusivity stands out against the backdrop of history. Humans have strong, primal tendencies towards tribalism. The negative aspects of these tendencies manifest in ways such

---

[28] Travis Mitchell, "On the Cusp of Adulthood and Facing an Uncertain Future: What We Know About Gen Z So Far," *Pew Research Center's Social & Demographic Trends Project* (blog), May 14, 2020, https://www.pewresearch.org/social-trends/2020/05/14/on-the-cusp-of-adulthood-and-facing-an-uncertain-future-what-we-know-about-gen-z-so-far-2/.

[29] "What Workforce Diversity Means for Gen Z," Monster, May 20, 2023, https://hiring.monster.com/resources/workforce-management/diversity-in-the-workplace/workforce-diversity-for-millennials/.

[30] Joelle Fredman, "75% of Gen Z Candidates Consider Company D&I Efforts When Deciding Whether to Apply," RippleMatch, September 29, 2022, https://ripplematch.com/insights/75-of-gen-z-candidates-consider-company-di-efforts-when-deciding-whether-to-apply/.

as ethnocentrism, aggressive patriotism, casteism, and xenophobia. We have seen these tendencies dictate the course of much of human history. Gen Z shows us a path beyond such tribalism, beyond even the mere absence of discrimination, to a sense of appreciation for differences. On the other hand, tribalism is now emerging in new ways that are equally strong, such as within the political right or the political left or within different identity groups. So, we cannot say that tribalism is gone, but we can appreciate the advancements, especially with regards to ethnicity.

To be effective listeners to this generation, we would have to abandon any monolithic approaches that have worked in the past. The formation of persons cannot be like a factory that produces items from the same mold. The person we are listening to may not come from the cultural background with which we grew up. They may not be familiar with all of the nuanced social behaviors and norms of a particular segment of society, and they may not care as much about them. Moreover, there are complex overlaps between cultures through migration or intermarriage, for example. The best approach is to ask clarifying questions and to do our best to understand the young person in the context of their background instead of our own. The increased level and positive recognition of diversity in Gen Z can hopefully motivate us to take more inside-out approaches, focusing on young people's interior growth in holiness and virtue more than on their behavioral conformity. In addition to all of the above, young people today rightly expect us to exemplify a welcoming spirit to people of diverse backgrounds. If we are perceived as dismissive or discriminatory towards people of different backgrounds, we will not hold much credibility in their eyes.

The future of mankind

These are some of the key characteristics of young people today. We may like or dislike them. They may cause us to rejoice or to weep. Regardless, these young people are the future of the world. And our calling is to serve them. Pope St. John Paul II wrote, "If [young people] turn to authority figures, they do so because they see in them a wealth of human warmth and a willingness to walk with them along the paths they are following."[31] Christ calls us to encounter their reality, to listen to them attentively, and to accompany them with love. As we strive to do so, we can all the more effectively help them reach the fullness of who they are called to be in Christ.

---

[31] Pope St. John Paul II, *Crossing the Threshold of Hope*, ed. Vittorio Messori, trans. Jenny McPhee and Martha McPhee (New York: Alfred A. Knopf, 1994), 121.

Key Points:

1. To listen well to young people, it is helpful to understand the unique characteristics of their generation, such as their beliefs, values, and priorities.

2. Young people prioritize work-life balance, personal development, and quality of life over financial success. They value meaningful work and ethical considerations when choosing employment. Listening to their noble aspirations and providing encouragement for a meaningful life can support their pursuit of purpose beyond monetary gain.

3. Young people face significant mental health challenges, including anxiety, depression, and distress. Understanding their struggles and offering empathic listening without perpetuating protectionism can empower them to navigate adversity through trust in God and their own inner resourcefulness.

4. Gen Zs are fluent in digital communication and can seamlessly integrate the various forms of digital and in-person communication. To effectively listen to them, we must be willing to participate to at least some degree in their ways of communicating, while also modeling an authentically human environment where they can express themselves and be loved without the pressure of being "interesting".

5. Gen Z is the most diverse generation, appreciating and actively seeking inclusivity in various aspects of society. They challenge us to be more diverse in our thinking and to focus more on genuine virtue than on social uniformity.

Reflection Questions:

1. What are some ways you can cultivate a deeper understanding of young people's context, values, and characteristics in order to listen to them effectively and connect with them on a meaningful level?

2. As you listen to young people, how can you authentically empathize with their mental health struggles, providing encouragement and support while avoiding the trap of overprotection or trying to solve their problems for them?

3. What are your fears about engaging with young people on the digital platforms where they communicate?

4. Is there anything you or your ministry/parish/institution is doing that could be a barrier to creating a safe and inclusive environment where young people from diverse backgrounds feel equally welcome?

5. In your interactions with young people who may be questioning their faith or not yet living morally sound lives, how can you gently and attentively listen to them while accompanying them on the journey of holiness?

CHAPTER 4

Choose the Right Listening Type

Stephen Covey famously identified five "levels of listening": ignoring, pretending, selective listening, attentive listening, and empathic listening.[1] These levels lie on a continuum that extends from not listening to truly listening. Covey's work has inspired many to realize that listening is not binary and that we all need to work at becoming better listeners. On the other hand, they imply that the goal is always empathic listening. There are in fact several *types* of listening, all of which are good in different contexts. Learning about the listening taxonomy can help us apply the right listening type(s) in a given situation.

Before we proceed, let us consider what listening itself is. Until now, we were employing an intuitive or basic understanding of listening. To study its practice and to derive its types, we stand in need of a technical definition. Listening may be defined as *the process of receiving, attending to, and assigning meaning to messages from others.*[2] In the first chapter, we mentioned that listening is more than hearing. In this technical definition, hearing is not even mentioned. The word used is receiving, which includes not only hearing, but also seeing and other senses as well. We want to pay attention to any and all sensory data that might help us comprehend the

---

[1] Stephen R. Covey, *The 7 Habits of Highly Effective People*, Electronic Edition (New York: RosettaBooks, 2009), 240; or see Stephen R. Covey, *The 8th Habit: From Effectiveness to Greatness*, Reprint edition (New York: Free Press, 2005), 192.

[2] Andrew D. Wolvin, *Listening* (Madison: Brown & Benchmark, 1996); see also Andrew D. Wolvin, "Listening, Understanding, and Misunderstanding," in *21st Century Communication: A Reference Handbook*, by William Eadie (2455 Teller Road, Thousand Oaks California 91320 United States: SAGE Publications, Inc., 2009), 137–46, https://doi.org/10.4135/9781412964005.n16.

message or intended meaning that someone is communicating to us accurately and precisely. Using our senses, we notice the words, body language, tone of voice, facial expression, and more. Listening is therefore a rich and complex process that begins with receiving a message.

Two aspects of communication and two types of listening

Since listening involves the receiving and processing of *messages*, we can determine the taxonomy of listening types based on the characteristic features of these messages. *There are two facets to every human message: the content aspect and the relational aspect.*[3] Sometimes, the content will be the more important of the two, such as when someone is giving directions. Other times, the relational aspect will be more important, such as when friends are catching up. So, while you will find both aspects in every

---

[3] Paul Watzlawick and Janet Beavin, "Some Formal Aspects of Communication," *American Behavioral Scientist* 10, no. 8 (June 26, 2023), https://doi.org/10.1177/0002764201000802.

message, the way in which we attend to these aspects will vary depending on the situation. This sets the stage for there being different types of listening.

When listening is focused on the content aspect of a message, it seeks out concepts, facts, and other forms of objective information. *Content-oriented listening*, also called cognitive listening, therefore largely depends on the intellect. If a young person is telling you about her research into various career options and lists out the pros and cons of each, you would likely employ content-oriented listening. On the other hand, listening that is focused on the relational aspect of a message attends to the speaker's emotions and experiences. It requires the listener to pay special attention, not only to *what* is being said, but *how* it is being said. *Relational listening*, also called empathic listening or people-oriented listening, constitutes an essential part of friendships, therapy, and various mentoring relationships. If a young person is telling you about his broken heart, you would likely attend to his message with relational listening.

As seen in the two examples above, our listening style should lean towards one or the other, the content aspect or the relational aspect, depending on the situation. Of course, it is possible that we misread the situation and apply the wrong kind of listening. Perhaps the young man with a broken heart was not looking for empathy at all but for practical help with the way forward. Or perhaps the young woman was hoping you would just be present as she expressed her attempts to navigate these decisions. We do our best to listen in the way that would be most helpful, but this often comes through adjustments made throughout the conversation. In general, the type of listening that you should employ in a particular context depends on the *goals* of the conversation.[4] It is often helpful

---

[4] Graham D. Bodie and Debra L. Worthington, "Listening Styles Profile-Revised (LSP-R)," in *The Sourcebook of Listening Research* (John Wiley & Sons, Ltd, 2017), 402–9, https://doi.org/10.1002/9781119102991.ch42.

to step back and assess these goals, both the other person's goals and your own. Is the person coming to you for clarity? Is your intention at this point to build trust? Once you become conscious of the goals of a conversation, choosing the appropriate style is relatively straightforward.

Two Facets of Listening

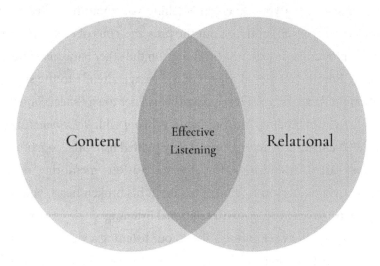

The three types of content-oriented listening

Content-oriented listening

Within our taxonomy of listening types, content-oriented listening can be subdivided further into three specific types.[5,6] Two of these types are directly relevant to the art of listening to young people. A third type is mentioned as something to avoid.

---

[5] See Bodie and Worthington.

[6] Rebecca D. Minehart, Benjamin B. Symon, and Laura K. Rock, "What's Your Listening Style?," *Harvard Business Review*, May 31, 2022, https://hbr.org/2022/05/whats-your-listening-style.

Analytical Listening attends to the full communication before forming an opinion about it. This type of listening, highly correlated with systematic thinking, will seek to gather all relevant information and to analyze it from every angle before drawing a conclusion. "I'm not sure yet,"

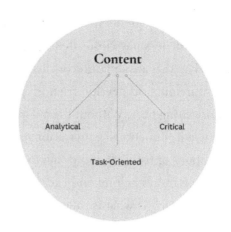

would be the typical response of an analytical listener who is asked to opine before they are ready. In the Christian life, many life situations, moral dilemmas, and vocational questions require this kind of listening. This is always preferred to the hasty application of judgment on the basis of an oversimplified construction of reality. When a young adult tells you that he intends to leave his girlfriend because he is considering the priesthood, you would want to know a lot more. What does 'considering the priesthood' mean for him? What events preceded his change of direction? How does he understand marriage and the priesthood? Without listening with a certain analytical curiosity, it would be impossible to accurately assess what is unfolding within him.

Critical Listening is not so much driven by curiosity as it is by the desire for coherence. It comes as second-nature for those with a high Need for Cognition (NfC), a quality correlated with general intelligence and with the enjoyment of effortful thinking for its own sake, such as in puzzle-solving.[7] This style is helpful in many contexts, especially where there is a

---

[7] John T. Cacioppo and Richard E. Petty, "The Need for Cognition," *Journal of Personality and Social Psychology* 42, no. 1 (1982): 116–31, https://doi.org/10.1037/0022-3514.42.1.116.

need to identify points that are inconsistent or inaccurate in a message. Critical listeners pay close attention and can help people notice parts of themselves that are still unreconciled. For example, a young person wants to venture out and develop friendships, but she also wants to avoid any risk of getting hurt. Without the aid of critical listeners, a person can get caught in dysfunctional patterns for years because of incongruities or false perceptions of reality that they fail to recognize. Of course, critical listening is not always helpful and can even be harmful, especially when empathic listening is what is called for. A person overcome with positive or negative emotion may not express their ideas with logical clarity, but this is normal and expected. People with high NfC will need to exercise restraint so as not to dissect everything they hear because of their proclivity for effortful thinking or their discomfort with temporary incoherence.

Task-Oriented Listening is something to *avoid* in the context of pastorally listening to young people. This type of listening aims to get to the "bottom-line" for the sake of completing a task. If the airline agent was explaining your options after the last flight home was unexpectedly canceled, you would be engaging in task-oriented listening. You would not be interested in hearing about the history of the airlines at that moment. "Get to the point," might be the words running through a task-oriented listener's mind. Because of its transactional nature, relevance of content is determined solely by its utility to the task at hand. When listening to young people pastorally, the young person should never be reduced to a task. If a formation advisor or spiritual director is meeting with someone either to check off a box or to "fix" their issues, this would result in task-oriented listening. Questions like "Did you meet the goal we set of socializing more this month?", depending on the context, may not convey genuine interest in the good of the person. The person may feel like a means for you to accomplish your agenda of changing the person in predetermined ways. Often, the young person will put up walls or subtly rebel as they instinctively seek to protect themselves from being reduced to a means. While task-oriented listening is well-suited for specific work-contexts, people who default to task-oriented listening in ordinary relationships usually exhibit verbal aggressiveness, lack of enjoyment in listening, and a lack of empathy.[8] Task-oriented listening is ill-suited to pastoral ministry because it is more about the listener and their goals than the one being listened to.

Relational listening in detail

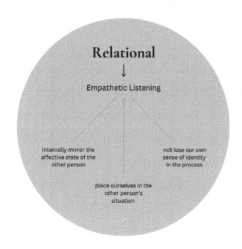

Content-oriented listening by itself would be entirely inadequate for human relationships and personal growth. After all, we are not merely information systems that relay data to each other. Even when the most practical information is shared, such as a restaurant recommendation, the communication involves a relational aspect. Friendships grow even through such small, matter-of-fact interactions. In addition to the relational aspect of all communication, relationships

---

[8] Bodie and Worthington, "Listening Styles Profile-Revised (LSP-R)." Note that the listening types used in this research are made through questionnaires that assess one's general tendencies. Thus, a person who is primarily a task-oriented listener is described as "socially callous." However, as mentioned above, in the narrow scope of urgent, task-dominant contexts, task-oriented listening can be positive.

themselves make up a large portion of what we communicate about. Think about how much time you spend talking about people and relationships, whether at home, in your ministry groups, or at work. We are inherently more relational than informational, and social dynamics affect us more primally and forcefully than ideas do. Moreover, we know that the highest human activity is *love*. Therefore, we would be truly oblivious to reality if we did not engage in relational listening.

At the center of relational listening is being-with or participation in another person's perspective, experience, and situation. We cannot be unaffected in this type of listening, as we might be with content-oriented listening. On the contrary, we want to empathically experience the affective state of the other person. *Empathy* has been defined as "a complex, imaginative process through which an observer simulates another person's situated psychological states while maintaining clear self–other differentiation."[9] Therefore, empathic listening requires that we (1) internally mirror the affective state of the other person, (2) place ourselves in the other person's situation as we listen, and (3) not lose our own sense of identity in the process.[10] We do not place ourselves in their situation to see how *we would feel* about it but how *the other person feels* about it. If a 24-year-old young man tells you he is considering switching his major again, empathic listening means imaginatively and affectively exploring what it is like *for him to experience* this confusion. You might struggle to relate to his level of indecision. You might even find it irritating. However, his subjective state of constant indecision is a reality, and we cannot flee from it. If empathic listening does not come naturally in a particular situation, asking

---

[9] Amy Coplan, "Will the Real Empathy Please Stand up? A Case for a Narrow Conceptualization," *The Southern Journal of Philosophy* 49, no. s1 (2011): 40–65, https://doi.org/10.1111/j.2041-6962.2011.00056.x.

[10] Elizabeth Segal et al., *Assessing Empathy*. (New York: Columbia University Press, 2017), chap. 1.

oneself, "What would I be feeling in this situation if I was him, if I experienced life the way he does?" or a similar question can help awaken this capacity.

The following abbreviated description from Carl Rogers eloquently captures the beauty of what empathic listening is.

> The way of being with another person which is termed empathic has several facets. It means entering the private perceptual world of the other and becoming thoroughly at home in it. It involves being sensitive, moment to moment, to the changing felt meanings which flow in this other person, to the fear or rage or tenderness or confusion or whatever, that he/she is experiencing... It includes communicating your sensings of his/her world... [and] frequently checking with him/her as to the accuracy of your sensings, and being guided by the responses you receive. You are a confident companion to the person in his/her inner world...
>
> To be with another in this way means that for the time being you lay aside the views and values you hold for yourself in order to enter another's world without prejudice. In some sense it means that you lay aside your self and this can only be done by a person who is secure enough in himself that he knows he will not get lost in what may turn out to be the strange or bizarre world of the other, and can comfortably return to his own world when he wishes.
>
> *Perhaps this description makes clear that being empathic is a complex, demanding, strong yet subtle and gentle way of being.*[11]

---

[11] Carl R. Rogers, "Empathic: An Unappreciated Way of Being," *The Counseling Psychologist* 5, no. 2 (June 1975): 2–10, https://doi.org/10.1177/00110000750-0500202.

As Christians, we have gained much from modern philosophical and psychological movements. We have learned to study and appreciate subjectivity like never before. At the same time, we are called to integrate these advances into the more foundational Christian worldview, that is, to always look at them from the perspective of faith. The Rogerian approach is brilliant, but it can also be harmful without an interior conviction about truth-objectivity. Empathic listening does not mean that we suspend our faith to appreciate the perspective of the other. But it does mean that we stretch ourselves, in and with Christ on the Cross, to encounter the other person genuinely rather than standing aloof and insulated within a Christian subculture. The Word became flesh and dwelt among us. Truth takes on a palatable and yet uncorrupted form when it is eager and ready to abide with the other, especially in the messiness of life. This is love and truth together (Eph 4:15).[12]

The best listening type

By understanding this taxonomy and the complementarity of the types, we can avoid the mistake of assuming that one type of listening is always the best. Many assume that the best type of listening is the one that they are naturally good at. Instead, the best type of listening is determined by the goals of a conversation and the needs of the young person being listened to. Moreover, these types are not rigid categories. Even within the same conversation, multiple types are often employed in different combinations and with varying emphases. In the end, growing in awareness

---

[12] Note that while ἀληθεύοντες in Eph 4:15 is often translated as "speaking the truth," ἀληθεύω is a verb form of truth. The verse can also be translated as "being truthful in love." In this context, we mean that one should stand firm in the interior conviction of truth while extending oneself generously through empathic listening.

about the different types of listening, their proper contexts, and our proclivities or struggles with each will help us as we strive to serve young people better through effective listening.

Now that you have understood the listening typology, find out which type of listening you lean most towards. Turn to the appendix to take Dr. Graham Bodie's **Personal Listening Style Profile Questionnaire** (special thanks to Dr. Bodie for sharing this with us!)

Key Points:

1. Listening is defined as the process of receiving, attending to, and assigning meaning to messages from others.

2. All messages have a content aspect and a relational aspect. Correspondingly, there are content-oriented and relational types of listening.

3. Content-oriented listening can be analytical, which is helpful for forming a holistic picture, or critical, which is helpful for identifying inconsistencies and inaccuracies. A third type, task-oriented listening, should be avoided in the context of accompanying young people.

4. Relational listening is exercised through empathy, which is the ability to experience another person's affective states while preserving one's own sense of self.

5. Christian accompaniment calls for truth and charity and therefore for both content-oriented and relational types of listening. While the best type of listening in a given context is determined by the goals of that conversation, ultimately all the types of listening are complementary.

Reflection Questions:

1. Which of the content-oriented listening types comes most naturally for you?

2. How do you demonstrate empathy in your listening and what strategies could you employ to enhance your empathic listening skills?

3. Reflecting on your own listening behavior, do you tend to lean more towards content-oriented or relational listening? Does this vary in different environments, such as family, ministry, or work? How does this impact your communication and relationships?

Chapter 5

Listen for What, How, and Why

"Why doesn't the Church support a woman's right to choose?" Suppose a young person walks up to you and asks you this question. By uttering these few words, he sets off a chain of processes in your body and mind. Your outer ear, like a funnel, directs the sound waves of his voice to your eardrum, which then vibrates in tandem with his vocal chords. These vibrations travel through your middle ear, creating pressure changes within the fluid-filled labyrinth of your inner ear. As the fluid moves around, it brushes against hair cells, and these transform the vibrations into electrical signals. The signals then make their way along the auditory nerve to the auditory cortex of your brain. Here, the sound-turned-electricity is now rapidly parsed for its various characteristics and communicated to other regions of your brain, such as your emotions and memory, to enable you to perceive the words, to interpret them, and to respond to them.

The Auditory Pathway

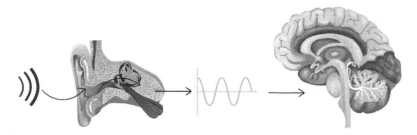

Deciphering the message

At a cognitive level, listening involves both *bottom-up* and *top-down* processing. In this spatial analogy, 'top' is the brain and 'bottom' is outside reality. The bottom-up dynamic represents the movement from physical reality to sensory stimuli and eventually to perception. A dripping faucet is a real, physical phenomenon. As the water drops splash against the basin, vibrations make their way through the air to your eardrum, setting off the process described above. Something similar happens with reflected light and your eyes. By the end, you are left with a nonphysical (i.e. a mental) representation of the physical reality. You can now commit this representation to memory, think about it, speak about it, and creatively connect it with other mental representations.

By contrast, top-down processing takes what we know from prior knowledge and maps it to what we perceive through bottom-up processing. This helps us fill in the blanks, read between the lines, contextualize what is being said, and predict and prepare for where the conversation might be going. For example, drawing from prior experience, we can intuit that someone opening with "I'm lost" is feeling lost about life and is not geospatially lost. We can begin to sense what the person might be feeling. Artificial intelligence language learning models have to mimic this intuition to seem realistic and useful to us. They do so by applying the most statistically likely context to the prompt you provide. ChatGPT responded to the prompt "I'm lost," with "I'm sorry to hear that you're feeling lost. It can be overwhelming when we find ourselves in a state of confusion or uncertainty..." Here, artificial intelligence mimics our ability to comprehend the literal meaning of words and then to make associations to countless thoughts and feelings from past experiences in order to determine the full breadth and context of what is being said. Without top-down processing, people would need to spell out everything in painful detail. This would render genuinely human communication impossible.

As we have seen, language interpretation is only possible with both bottom-up and top-down processing. Returning to the example of the young man above, when you perceive his words, tone, facial expression,

and posture, that is bottom-up processing. When you start drawing connections to past experiences of people who berated the Church and so find yourself being defensive, that is from top-down processing. Or, if you draw connections to your own adolescent struggles and become gentle and compassionate, that too comes from top-down processing. These two dynamics of processing converge to formulate one *three-dimensional message*. The more you pay attention, the more your comprehension will become clearer along these three dimensions:

- You understand (a) *what* people are saying.
- You notice (b) *how* they are saying (a).
- Then, from (a), (b), and prior experiences/knowledge, you determine (c) *why* they are saying (a).

Even when we are barely conscious of it, our brains do an excellent job of determining the *what*, *how*, and *why* of communication.[1] But when we do become conscious of it, we can develop these abilities deliberately and become much better listeners.

---

[1] Robert P. Spunt, "Mirroring, Mentalizing, and the Social Neuroscience of Listening," *International Journal of Listening* 27, no. 2 (May 1, 2013): 62, https://doi.org/10.1080/10904018.2012.756331.

Concentrate on what

If you concentrate on "wind" for a few seconds, you will notice where your mind takes you. Perhaps you recall the feeling of wind against your face, or the way it moves your clothes. Maybe you recall a place of breathtaking beauty and gusty winds. Or you remember learning about how it is caused by hot air rising and creating an area of low pressure behind it. Maybe you have a specific memory involving wind. To the mind, a word is never one thing. It is a series of associations to meanings, feelings, and experiences, something incredibly rich and multifaceted. When you hear a word, these associations begin to activate with varying intensities. If a young person describes a religious experience on a hiking trip and says to you, "I reached the top of the mountain and felt the Lord's presence in the wind," many such associations will automatically become present to you as you listen. This enables you to understand what they are talking about, as well as to empathize with their experience. You will also be able to draw connections to other experiences that they have shared with you in the past. The level to which these connections surface for you is directly proportional to the level of attention you give.[2,3] The Holy Spirit works through this natural process, if we are attentive, to remind you of important details or to help you notice small details of great significance and ask more about it. In certain cases, the Holy Spirit will work through special gifts to help you make new associations that are not directly drawn from prior knowledge (cf. 1 Cor 12:4-11; 1 Cor 14:1-5,24).

---

[2] Pan-tong Yao et al., "Cortical Ensemble Activity Discriminates Auditory Attentional States," *Molecular Brain* 12, no. 1 (October 17, 2019): 80, https://doi.org/10.1186/s13041-019-0502-z.

[3] Gioia De Franceschi and Tania Rinaldi Barkat, "Task-Induced Modulations of Neuronal Activity along the Auditory Pathway," *Cell Reports* 37, no. 11 (December 14, 2021), https://doi.org/10.1016/j.celrep.2021. 110115.

Good listeners try their best not to miss any part of what is being said. This happens through paying attention and avoiding distractions. In some contexts, writing notes during the conversation or after the conversation can be helpful, assuming the person consents to it.[4] One of our authors, while serving as a seminary formation advisor, found that occasionally consulting his notes enabled him to draw connections for the seminarian that extended over the span of months or years. Whether from notes or memory, it is often beneficial to highlight correlations, contrasts, patterns, and trends. For one, it shows that you have been listening to what the person has been saying. It also allows the young person to make greater sense of what is happening within them. "I remember the last time we met you said that you were not feeling motivated about life, but now you're describing so many exciting prospects. This is wonderful to hear. What changed for you?" A simple prompt, comparing what they said at another time with what they are saying now, can help them recognize their own growth, regression, or stagnation.

If you are someone with heavy top-down processing, keeping your attention fixed on the *words* that they are saying will keep you grounded. Remember that there is plenty of time in conversations, and there is no rush to make sense of it all at once. Being patient and curious enables you to arrive at true comprehension without making large and error-prone leaps. Rather than inferring things too early and overusing intuition, practice the technique of suspending judgments and of treating them in the meantime as mere 'possibilities'. Only a fraction of the possible interpretations will prove true. For the rest, you will let them go as easily as they came. If a young woman says, "I struggle to experience God as a loving Father," your mind may leap to an explanation. "She must have a broken relationship with her dad." Consider this as merely one among many possibilities as you continue to listen to exactly *what* she is saying. It would

---

[4] See more on note-taking in Chapter 7.

be especially unwise to reflect this interpretation back to her, even through a question, like, "Did you have a difficult relationship with your father?" This would distract her from what she was trying to communicate, and, worse, could misdirect her self-reflection. In a similar way, the undiscerning and immoderate use of the aforementioned spiritual gifts can work contrary to the virtues of listening as well. Remember, there is no rush to come to a judgment. As more details emerge through listening, as you pay attention to *what* they are saying, your natural intuition will become more accurate, and any spiritual intuitions will be further tested or refined.

Notice how

Knowing what is said is only part of the puzzle. We need to pay attention to *how* it was said as well. There are numerous ways in which the brain's audiovisual processing systems are equipped to help us ascertain the manner in which something is said. Intonation, for example, is a basic characteristic that always accompanies words and influences their meaning. Intonation sits at the boundary of verbal and nonverbal communication. To decipher intonation, there are neurons in your brain's auditory cortex that respond to tonal fluctuations relative to each speaker's baseline pitch.[5] This is how you know whether someone is asking or telling you something. "The elevator is that way" and "The elevator is that way?" are identical when spoken except for intonation, and yet they have very different meanings. Whether a child with a high-pitched voice or an adult male says these words, these neurons automatically detect the relative change in pitch to help you identify the nuances of meaning. Think of how

---

[5] C. Tang, L. S. Hamilton, and E. F. Chang, "Intonational Speech Prosody Encoding in the Human Auditory Cortex," *Science* 357, no. 6353 (August 25, 2017): 797–801, https://doi.org/10.1126/science.aam8577.

many different meanings these five words can have when they are said with different pitch inflections:

Inflection Variation	Meaning
The *elevator* is that way.	Not the stairs.
The elevator *is* that way.	It really is that way!
The elevator is *that* way.	You're going the wrong way.
The elevator is that way?	Are you sure it is that way?

Unlike English, many languages are inherently tonal, which means that the same sequence of phonemes used with different intonations constitute different words.[6] This is why intonation is considered to be a form of both verbal and nonverbal communication.[7] In certain cases, it changes the linguistic meaning and so is considered verbal communication. Usually, these are indicated by symbols, such as punctuation or italics, or are represented by distinct characters in tonal languages. In other cases, intonation reflects feeling or *how* something is said. In these cases, intonation belongs to the broader category of nonverbal communication.

Though we communicate through words, our words are not detached ideas. They are *enfleshed*, so to speak, because we communicate them

---

[6] Languages include Mandarin, Thai, Punjabi, Igbo, and numerous others. For example, in Igbo: óké = male, ókè = boundary, òkè = share/portion, óké = rat (https://www.igbovillagesquare.com/2020/12/ igbo-tone.html).

[7] David P. Snow, "Gesture and Intonation Are 'Sister Systems' of Infant Communication: Evidence from Regression Patterns of Language Development," *Language Sciences (Oxford, England)* 59 (January 2017): 180–91, https://doi.org/ 10.1016/j.langsci.2016.10.005.

through our bodies. When we speak, our tone, volume, pace, gestures, facial expressions, and posture all betray our underlying feelings. Are these emotional characteristics mere embellishments, added effects to dramatize our true, logically coherent message? More often than not, we are much less logical than we would like to believe. Desires, fears, and relational dynamics that we experience as human beings are often more powerful than our rational thoughts. Sometimes, the feelings *are* the message, and our thoughts and words are unwittingly at their service. Suppose the young man with the question was anxious and afraid about how to handle his girlfriend's pregnancy. *How* he asks his question would be just as important as his words, if not more important. Nonverbal signals contextualize words, and sometimes so much so that they unveil their true meaning over and against their logical facade.

Nonverbal cues naturally accompany the spoken word because the person who speaks does so through their body. Simultaneously, we as listeners do not upload spoken words directly into our cognitive brain. The enfleshed word that we hear is received through our own bodies. It travels from one embodied person to another. Because of this, we perceive nonverbal cues that we may not even be aware of. Your first reaction would not be to think, "I recognize that his voice is louder and higher pitched than usual." You *experience* these nonverbal cues. In a way, you can feel his agitation in your own body. Paying attention to what you experience as the listener is an excellent way to notice how a message is being communicated, even though your feelings can also be the result of intrapersonal factors.

Functional neuroimaging has given us important clues to how this process takes place. In a series of experiments, scientists first observed the brains of monkeys as they carried out ordinary tasks, such as reaching for food. Then, they observed their brains as they watched *other* monkeys reaching for food. Remarkably, they found that some of the same neurons were activated in either case.[8] These audiovisual *mirror neurons* have been discovered in human beings as well, and they extend to applications beyond reaching for food. Neurons that activate in your brain when you smile or frown, for example, also activate when you see someone else smile or frown.[9] This is part of the reason that you feel pleasant when someone smiles at you, before you even think about the fact that they are smiling at you. There are still many unknowns about the Mirror Neuron System (MNS), but we can intuit that through the MNS (and the other aspects of our brain that are equipped for social cognition and empathy), *listeners to some extent experience what the speaker is experiencing.* What better way to understand the rich and nuanced context of another person's words than to feel what they are feeling? When a young woman comes to you racked with guilt, you will feel some of what she is feeling just by the look in her eyes or the tone of her voice. The way that God has richly designed the human person, our brains automatically capture this rich context, the *how*, that surrounds human language.[10]

Knowing how the MNS works also provides us with opportunities for growth in listening. In experiments where listeners were asked to pay attention not just to *what* was being said but *how* it was being said, their

---

[8] G. di Pellegrino et al., "Understanding Motor Events: A Neurophysiological Study," *Experimental Brain Research* 91, no. 1 (1992): 176–80, https://doi.org/10.1007/BF00230027.

[9] Roy Mukamel et al., "Single Neuron Responses in Humans during Execution and Observation of Actions," *Current Biology : CB* 20, no. 8 (April 27, 2010): 750–56, https://doi.org/10.1016/j.cub.2010.02.045.

[10] The complete absence of nonverbal expression and perception is one of the major limitations of textual communication, such as SMS or social media. However, there are ways to mitigate this deficiency. See the Digital Generation section of Chapter 3.

MNS was observably more active.[11] This is great news. A simple self-reminder to pay attention to how people are saying what they are saying will help activate this incredible gift. Experiencing what the speaker is experiencing yields a more interiorized and experiential knowledge of what they are telling you, which is at the heart of being an excellent listener.

In these and countless other ways, by God's gracious design, we are very well equipped to be able to perceive not just the meaning of a person's words but the manner in which their words are spoken. Noticing *how* a person is communicating is an essential part of the ministry of listening.

Determine why

As we listen, we do our best to determine *why*, that is, to ascertain the reason for a person's communication. Sometimes people are explicit about their reasons, in which case the reason is communicated verbally and directly. This is often the case with assertive people. It is also possible when trust is established and you can ask the person for the reason. If there is trust, you can respond to the question "Why doesn't the Church support a woman's right to choose?" with:

> "I'm glad you felt comfortable bringing this important and sensitive question to me. I can assure you that Christ, through his Church, desires nothing but the best for all of us, and that his wise but often challenging teachings about love, life, and everything else are all designed for our benefit. I'd love to share more. Could you give me some more context to your question? What made you think about this question today?"

---

[11] Spunt, "Mirroring, Mentalizing, and the Social Neuroscience of Listening," 65–66.

Sometimes giving the person a chance to provide the reason will make all the difference for how the conversation proceeds. Knowing the *why* helps you interpret everything that the person says in the right context. In other cases, people will not provide a reason explicitly or verbally. Here, tone and the other nonverbal signals are important clues, as described above. Certain tones and facial expressions unambiguously communicate underlying reasons, while others only give you a range of possibilities.

There are times when people will not give you the real reason verbally and their tone and other nonverbal signals will be ambiguous, cryptic, or even deceptive. In these cases, prior *specific knowledge* about the person and situation, together with *generalized knowledge* gained through life experiences and learning, work together to help you infer the reason based on just a few subtle indicators. Prior specific knowledge about the person

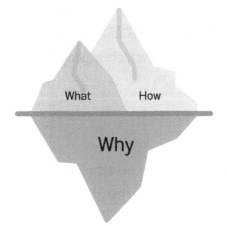

comes through attentiveness to patterns that emerge slowly over the course of the relationship. Most of the time, a person's *why* is consistent with what you know the person to be like. If you already know the young person above and know that he is sensitive to perceived injustices, you would infer that his reason for asking has to do with this concern. Generalized knowledge comes through life experience and other methods of learning, such as reading or professional training. This is why ongoing education is highly recommended for spiritual directors, youth ministers, seminary formators, therapists, and others who help people through listening. There are general patterns we can learn to recognize, which can help us ascertain underlying reasons.

The *why* of communication is like the submerged portion of an iceberg. *Why* someone is shouting angrily is usually far more significant than *what* they are shouting. *Why* a young person is telling you about her disdain for the Church may be far more important than her tone. Is she hurting? Is she testing you? Simply pausing and asking oneself "Why?" can make a significant difference. Of course, an inadequate basis for an inference or the projection of our own issues will result in a wrong inference. This is the danger of when top-down processing becomes too dominant, as mentioned above. When we are unsure, it is always best to ask clarifying questions.

Through top-down and bottom-up processing working together and with a level of intentionality, we can learn to pay close attention to the *what, how,* and *why* of communication. God has blessed us with the psychophysiological mechanisms to engage in rich and multi-layered communication. Growing in awareness about these gifts and using them more consciously will help us cultivate them for the greater benefit of the young people we serve.

Key Points:

1. Listening is a complex process that combines sensory perception (bottom-up processing) with interpretation based on prior knowledge and experience (top-down processing). Both types of processing are necessary for listening.

2. Every communication has three dimensions: what, how, and why. Attentive listening ascertains what the person is saying, how they are saying it, and why they are saying it.

3. *What* they are saying is determined by the words they say. A word does not signify a singular reality but has many associated meanings, experiences, and feelings. As we listen attentively to the

words, we do our best to decipher their intended meaning with its appropriate depth.

4. *How* the person is speaking is determined by nonverbal cues, such as intonation, facial expression, and body language. Nonverbal cues provide additional context and can even substantially alter the meaning of a message. Certain natural mechanisms enable us to experience what the other person is feeling even before it comes to our conscious awareness. At the same time, actively paying attention to how the person is communicating will strengthen our empathic awareness.

5. To fully understand the message, we need to determine *why* they are saying it. This underlying reason or intention is sometimes explicitly stated, while in other cases, it may need to be inferred through prior knowledge, context, and careful observation of nonverbal signals.

6. To avoid inadequately substantiated inferences and projection, we must learn to suspend judgments and treat them as mere possibilities at first. As we patiently listen, these possibilities will be tested and proven true or false.

Reflection Questions:

1. Do you consider yourself stronger at bottom-up or top-down processing? What benefits and challenges does this provide you with?

2. When listening to a young person, how well do you listen to *what* exactly they are saying? What practices help you stay more attentive?

3. How well do you perceive *how* a young person is communicating to you? What practices help you experience what they are feeling as you listen?

4. When listening to a young person, do you consider *why* they are saying what they are saying? What practices can help you develop this habit?

5. Do you ever make hasty inferences out of impatience? How can you cultivate a greater sense of patience and create an environment that encourages open and unhurried dialogue?

CHAPTER 6

A List of Barriers and False Forms of Listening

Listening is about encountering and making space for the other person with an open ear, mind, and heart. There are however some behaviors that significantly hinder this process. In this chapter, we want to examine the many kinds of *barriers* that would prevent listening, as well as *false forms* of listening. By learning about them, our hope is to become more self-aware, to identify any counterproductive tendencies we may have, and to gradually learn to keep them in check.

In Chapter 4, we identified two primary types of listening: content-oriented listening and relational listening. Both of these higher-level listening categories depend upon a foundational listening type called discriminative listening.

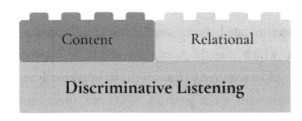

Discriminative listening allows us to identify words and nonverbal signals, to distinguish between syllables or tones, and to filter out irrelevant audiovisual stimuli. At any given moment, the brain receives countless sensory stimuli. This underlying form of listening enables us to focus on the stimuli of interest, so that we can receive the message and pass it along for higher-level processing. Discriminative, content-oriented, and relational listening can each be negatively affected by specific behaviors, conditions, mindsets, and distractions. In general, we have called these 'barriers to listening'. While it is not possible to be a perfect listener, we can work to minimize these barriers over time.

Barriers to discriminative listening

Physiological and Cognitive Barriers: The first obstacles to discriminative listening are physiological and cognitive. These include hearing problems and attention deficit disorders. People with sensory processing disorders (SPDs) cannot easily focus on the intended stimuli, such as a person's words. They can

also find it difficult to discriminate between similar sounding words and variations of intonation, which then impairs their ability to interpret words and emotions. The effort required to listen well can be mentally and physically exhausting, even with much practice. SPDs can affect those with mental health issues, such as ADHD, anxiety, depression, and autism. Those who have difficulties with discrimination of sounds should seek professional and medical help to identify the nature of the problem and seek out therapeutic options and tools. In addition to SPDs, lack of sleep, physical pain, tiredness, and other physiological factors can diminish discriminative listening.

Environmental Barriers: Background noise, such as conversations, traffic, or machinery, can create distractions and interfere with the clarity of the speaker's words, as can the acoustics of a room with reverberation, echoes, or poor sound insulation. Priests at youth events are often asked to hear confessions with background music playing to protect the penitents' privacy. If quieter spaces are not available, the most predictable and perhaps uninteresting type of background sound or music possible should be used because 'novel' sounds automatically redirect your brain's attention.[1] Visual distractions in the environment, such as bright lights, moving objects, or clutter, can do the same. As social creatures, we can be awfully curious about what people are doing around us. Setting up the right environment for listening should include positioning your chairs thoughtfully, for example, to avoid being distracted by people who are walking by. Creating a quiet and focused environment free from unnecessary interruptions will always support better listening.

Digital-Environmental Barriers: For phone or video calls, poor connections and bad sound quality can compromise discriminative listening. Sound quality can easily be remedied by investing in good earphones/headphones with a built-in microphone and noise cancellation.[2] The built-in speaker and microphone of one's phone or laptop should be avoided. Looking at one's phone or smartwatch notifications does not facilitate genuine, interpersonal listening. While it may be acceptable practice in certain kinds of work environments, in the context of listening and encountering, it distracts us from the person before us.[3] Even when we do

---

[1] David Pérez-González, Manuel S. Malmierca, and Ellen Covey, "Novelty Detector Neurons in the Mammalian Auditory Midbrain," *The European Journal of Neuroscience* 22, no. 11 (December 2005): 2879–85, https://doi.org/10.1111/j.1460-9568.2005.04472.x.

[2] Look for products with *Active Noise Cancellation* if you are in particularly noisy environments.

[3] Social media has become an aggressive competition for attention and young people often feel the pressure to present an interesting persona to be noticed and liked by others (see Chapter 3). Giving young people our undivided attention relieves them of this pressure, gives them the freedom to be themselves, and models a more authentic way of being in relationship.

not look at our devices, the quiet vibrations of our phone or smartwatch can distract even the most experienced listeners, as our minds begin to wonder what the call or message might be about.

Speech-Perceptibility Barriers: Some barriers depend more on the person who is speaking than on the listener, such as the speaker's volume, diction, accent, or fluency. In these cases, we will have to kindly ask the young person to speak slowly and loudly. When it comes to non-native speakers, we might desire the person to improve their pronunciation, but of course this is beyond our control. Fortunately, it is well-documented that *we* can improve our comprehension of non-native speech simply by increasing our exposure to it. Our understanding will improve if we either spend more time listening to a particular, foreign accent or we spend more time listening to foreign accents in general.[4] In the meantime, conversing with such a young person will undoubtedly require more cognitive processing costs and induce fatigue. We may find ourselves in need of breaks because of the heavy top-down processing work required to infer what was meant each time we cannot decipher a word definitively.[5]

Barriers to content-oriented listening

Controlling the Narrative: What makes it difficult to calmly and patiently listen to someone who is presenting an unorthodox or erroneous viewpoint? When St. Stephen testified to his faith, saying "Behold, I see the heavens opened, and the Son of Man standing at the right hand of God," his listeners "cried out with a loud voice and *stopped their ears* and rushed together at him. Then they cast him out of the city and stoned him" (Acts

---

[4] Melissa M. Baese-Berk, Drew J. McLaughlin, and Kevin B. McGowan, "Perception of Non-Native Speech," *Language and Linguistics Compass* 14, no. 7 (2020): e12375, https://doi.org/10.1111/lnc3.12375.

[5] Shiri Lev-Ari, "Comprehending Non-Native Speakers: Theory and Evidence for Adjustment in Manner of Processing," *Frontiers in Psychology* 5 (2015).

7:56-58a). While we do not pick up stones, we may perhaps stop our ears when we hear something we do not like. Once we sense that a conversation is going somewhere we do not want, our defenses come up and we start preparing for a counterattack. In the polarized times we live in, the inability to

Barriers to Content Oriented Listening

Controlling the Narrative

Superficial Distractions

Intellectual Insecurity

Mental Disorganization

Closeness-Communication Bias

listen calmly is practically celebrated as a virtue.[6,7] Pope Francis writes, "The ability to sit down and listen to others, typical of interpersonal encounters, is paradigmatic of the welcoming attitude shown by those who transcend narcissism and accept others, caring for them and welcoming them into their lives. Yet today's world is largely a deaf world... Halfway through, we interrupt him and want to contradict what he has not even finished saying."[8]

If we are honest with ourselves, we are often *afraid to lose control of where the conversation goes.*[9] We try to interject, to steer the conversation in the right direction. We can hardly sit still when someone is expressing

---

[6] Greg Lukianoff and Jonathan Haidt, *The Coddling of the American Mind: How Good Intentions and Bad Ideas Are Setting Up a Generation for Failure* (New York: Penguin Books, 2018), chap. 6.

[7] Dan Crenshaw, *Fortitude: American Resilience in the Era of Outrage* (New York: Twelve, 2020), chap. Introduction.

[8] Pope Francis, *Fratelli Tutti: Encyclical on Fraternity and Social Friendship* (New London, CT: Twenty-Third Publications, 2020), 48.

[9] Kate Murphy, *You're Not Listening: What You're Missing and Why It Matters* (New York, NY: Celadon Books, 2021), 111.

a problematic opinion, such as a young person who is talking about the benefits of recreational drug usage. This may stimulate feelings of anger because of how wrong or immoral we believe they are and how harmful their opinions may be. Simultaneously, we feel a passionate assurance of our own correctness.[10] We can be free of the fear of losing control if we remind ourselves that:

1) There will be time to respond, but now is the time to listen, both analytically and critically.

2) Giving the young person time to fully express their viewpoint to you will not cause their potential error to gain traction or better footing in the world.

3) There will be aspects of truth in what the young person is saying and probably even something that can be learned, if we listen well.

4) Listening is not a show of endorsement for an idea. It is an expression of reverence for the other person as being worthy of respect, which is especially important for young people whose viewpoints are often unwelcome.

Remember, even the most egregious and unacceptable ideas are just that – someone else's ideas. No harm is done by letting go of control for the sake of genuine listening and understanding. On the contrary, we can strengthen the relationship through listening to make mutual understanding and dialogue possible. Authentic listening involves taking risks, letting yourself be in a situation where you do not have all the answers, and entering into the unknowable mystery of another person. It involves moving past an overly simplistic and falsely reassuring, black-and-white

---

[10] Julia A. Minson and Charles A. Dorison, "Why Is Exposure to Opposing Views Aversive? Reconciling Three Theoretical Perspectives," *Current Opinion in Psychology* 47 (October 1, 2022): 101435, https://doi.org/10.1016/j.copsyc.2022. 101435.

vision of the world, to accept that reality is full of important values held in tension.[11] Just as traveling to a new place can be enjoyable in all its unpredictability, listening without controlling can be exciting and enriching. Often, the best conversations happen when we allow ourselves to take this risk of venturing out beyond the safe confines of agreeable topics.[12]

Superficial Distractions: It is easy to get distracted by the style or delivery of the speaker rather than the substance of their message. St. Thomas More, in his 1523 petition for free speech, the first ever in history, wrote: "It often happeneth, that likewise as much folly is uttered with painted polished speeches, so many boisterous and rude in language see deep indeed, and give right substantial counsel..."[13] Paying excessive attention to qualities like the speaker's misuse of a word, grammar, accent, appearance, or mannerisms can divert your attention away from the content or substance they present. Whatever else our mind obsesses over, no matter how much we feel justified in dwelling on it, is a distraction from listening. The mental discipline of listening requires that we do not indulge distractions but rather bring our attention back to what the person is saying. Additionally, judgments based on superficial characteristics will typically introduce bias and distort comprehension. The fact that a young woman uses slang words or a young man has his hair a particular way does not discredit them and should not hinder our ability to genuinely listen to what they are saying.

Intellectual Insecurity: When individuals feel confident about their ability to comprehend another person, they are more likely to actively engage in

---

[11] See William F. Lynch SJ, *Images of Hope: Imagination as Healer of the Hopeless* (University of Notre Dame Pess, 1974), chap. 5.

[12] Murphy, *You're Not Listening*, 23,43.

[13] William Roper, "The Life of Sir Thomas More," Fordham University, 1556.

listening, and they tend to approach conversations with a positive mindset. Confidence enhances focus, attention, and overall receptivity to the other person's message.[14] On the other hand, insecurity about one's ability to listen and understand, together with the sense of self-consciousness that follows, has the reverse effect. If you fear that you are not smart enough to understand someone, you are more likely to fail to understand them. Likewise, frequently stepping out of other-centered listening to ask yourself, "Am I doing this right?" will distract you from the sustained attention required to comprehend complex and nuanced ideas. Because it distracts you from listening, paradoxically, asking the question will often lead you to "doing this wrong".

Mental Disorganization: One of the reasons that listening can be challenging is that speakers do not typically organize their thoughts in advance and filter out irrelevant information. A young person may go off on many tangents or dwell upon extraneous details. This is quite natural and should not be seen as a bad thing, unless it becomes excessive. For example, a young person relating her experience at a retreat may start by talking about her first impressions, switch into rehashing one of the talks she heard, mention the beauty of the liturgies, and then begin talking about her inner experience. Internally prioritizing and organizing what is said helps the listener stay focused and attentive instead of becoming mentally exhausted or lost in the details. Knowing and gently reminding ourselves of what we are primarily listening for can help facilitate mental organization.

Closeness-Communication Bias: Close relationships naturally involve deep mutual understanding. However, they also pose a risk to listening because

---

[14] Elham Kavandi, "To Prompt It: How Does Self-Confidence Affect Listening Skill?," *International Journal of Innovation and Research in Educational Sciences* 9, no. 1 (2022).

we have a tendency to overestimate how well we understand a person to whom we are close.[15] Rather than paying careful attention to what the person is saying, we rely too heavily on top-down processing and make inaccurate inferences.[16] Imagine you have been accompanying a young man for several years, and you have seen him lose money on risky business ventures before. As soon as he begins to talk about a new business idea, you may struggle to keep an open mind and to listen patiently, analytically, and critically, but without bias. The fallacy behind this barrier is that human beings are unchanging and predictable. As the journalist Kate Murphy writes, "Relying on the past to understand someone in the present is doomed to failure."[17] The Second Vatican Council beautifully affirms that man is a *mystery* who is constantly being revealed even unto himself. Closeness or familiarity does not exhaust this mystery, and we should always stand ready to be surprised by what comes forth from the interiority of a young person.

Barriers to relational listening

Objectivity Bias/Affective Insecurity: Sir Arthur Conan Doyle's *Sherlock Holmes* artfully presents the tension between the merits of pure reason and the value of empathy. This theme continues to attract attention in modern TV shows like *Sherlock* and *House M.D.* The question is foundational: what is more helpful to people in crisis, empathy or solving their problems? If we believe that subjectivity and emotions are of minor sig-

---

[15] Kenneth Savitsky et al., "The Closeness-Communication Bias: Increased Egocentrism among Friends versus Strangers," *Journal of Experimental Social Psychology* 47, no. 1 (January 2011): 269–73, https://doi.org/10.1016/j.jesp.2010.09.005.

[16] See Chapter 4.

[17] Murphy, *You're Not Listening*, 50.

nificance, we will neglect people's affective states. We will focus on analyses and solutions and miss the opportunity just to *be with* the person in need. In many ways, it comes down to the question of whether love itself is valuable. The modern skeptic might say that love only makes us feel better and that it is better to have our problems actually solved through technical advancement. On the contrary, we believe that love is the greatest virtue and fulfills the *greatest longing and need* of the human person. It is the purpose of our existence. The skeptic is blind to this. At the same time, a listener who is insecure about their ability to be affectively present to another person practically ends up in the same position as the skeptic. The affec-

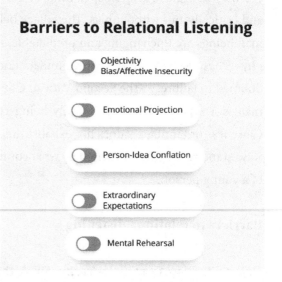

Barriers to Relational Listening

- Objectivity Bias/Affective Insecurity
- Emotional Projection
- Person-Idea Conflation
- Extraordinary Expectations
- Mental Rehearsal

tively insecure listener will avoid touching on unsolvable areas of regret or loss, for example, because they do not know how to just be with someone. "The Latin word *con-solatio*, 'consolation', expresses this beautifully. It suggests being with the other in his solitude, so that it ceases to be solitude."[18] Objectivity-bias and affective-insecurity prevent people from loving and being with others through listening.

Emotional Projection: Empathy is foundational to good listening. However, we can sometimes think we are aware of what another person feels,

---

[18] Pope Benedict XVI, *Spe Salvi*, 2023, 38, https://www.vatican.va/content/benedict-xvi/en/encyclicals/documents/hf_ben-xvi_enc_20071130_spe-salvi.html.

when all we are doing is attributing our own feelings to them. Indeed, much or most of what we consider empathy may be projection.[19] People consider listeners who are strongly moved by emotion to be highly empathic, for example, but this is not necessarily the case. Hypothetically, someone who cries with you when you experience loss might actually be projecting their own unresolved sense of loss. A disproportionate emotional response is often a good indication of projection. For this reason, *being present* to another cannot be a purely *affective* activity. In fact, neurocognitively, such interactions clearly involve the coactivation of both the *affective* and the *cognitive* processes of the brain.[20] One must truly *understand* the other person to *feel* what he or she is feeling accurately. Asking open-ended questions and then listening attentively, with affective sensitivity, will ensure that empathy does not become projection but remains other-centric.

Person-Idea Conflation: The philosopher Karl Popper believed that human beings produced knowledge in a way analogous to how spiders produce webs. Once a theory is formulated or once a book is written, it has a separate existence from its creator.[21] There should be in our minds a healthy separation between people and their ideas that allows us to befriend people even when we reject their ideas. This separation also allows us to *listen for what is deeper than their ideas.* First of all, the fact that a person ex-

---

[19] I. E. Bender and A. H. Hastorf, "On Measuring Generalized Empathic Ability (Social Sensitivity)," *The Journal of Abnormal and Social Psychology* 48, no. 4 (1953): 503–6, https://doi.org/10.1037/h0054486.

[20] Matthias Schurz et al., "Toward a Hierarchical Model of Social Cognition: A Neuroimaging Meta-Analysis and Integrative Review of Empathy and Theory of Mind," *Psychological Bulletin* 147, no. 3 (March 2021): 293–327, https://doi.org/10.1037/bul0000303.

[21] Jonathan Rauch, *The Constitution of Knowledge: A Defense of Truth* (D.C.: Brookings Institution, 2021), 86.

presses an idea passionately does not mean that they have thoroughly em-
braced that idea. Certain ideas give them a sense of belongingness to a
special group or protect them from being ostracized (perhaps using preferred pronouns, for example). Other ideas serve as desperate rationaliza-
tions for their moral struggles. At such an exploratory stage of life, die-
hard convictions can change like the wind. Therefore, preoccupation with
someone's ideas can be a major distraction to relational listening. If you
are listening to a young person arguing with you about why there is nothing wrong with premarital relationships, ask yourself, "What are they
searching for?" Or if you listen to a new seminarian who rejects the teach-
ings of the Second Vatican Council, instead of arguing for hours on end,
ask yourself, "Where is his anger coming from?" Even while we must respect a person's ideas enough to listen to them, we simultaneously know
that a person is not their ideas. An open-minded curiosity about *the person who holds these ideas* and *how they came to arrive at them* can help one
overcome this barrier to relational listening.

Extraordinary Expectations: Listening requires a cultivated sensitivity for
finding delight in the most ordinary and gradual. Most of what we have
become, we became slowly. We gradually grew into who we are today
through each hour of prayer, each class period in school, each conversation, each confession, etc. When listening to a young person, we should
not expect fireworks. While dramatic shifts do take place in a person's life
at key junctures, a great deal happens through the gentle and patient work
of the Spirit. Listening with expectations of extraordinariness will distract
us from the relational wonder of each conversation. Of course, we should
qualitatively guide conversations towards becoming more genuine and
personal wherever possible. But if we lose interest in the ordinary, we must
examine whether our listening shows genuine interest in the other.

Mental Rehearsal: When we are anxious about how we are going to respond to someone, we might start mentally formulating a response before they finish speaking. Effectively, we stop listening so that we can respond better, which is absurd! If our only intention is to win a debate, there is perhaps some room for this strategy. But when accompanying young people, the more we listen to what is being said, the more meaningfully and effectively we will be able to respond. Resisting the urge to mentally rehearse also means accepting that *what we say will be imperfect.*[22] Being imperfect in conversation may in fact be an advantage. It shows our sincerity and humanity. As we try to communicate, it gives the other an opportunity to know who we are, not just what we are saying, and this can strengthen the effectiveness of our communication.[23]

Barriers to Listening

Discriminative	Content-Oriented	Relational
Physiological and Cognitive	Controlling the Narrative	Objectivity Bias/Affective Insecurity
Environmental	Superficial Distractions	Emotional Projection
Digital-Environmental	Intellectual Insecurity	Person-Idea Conflation
Speech-Perceptibility	Mental Disorganization	Extraordinary Expectations
	Closeness-Communication Bias	Mental Rehearsal

---

[22] Murphy, *You're Not Listening,* 74.

[23] Heinz Kohut and Charles B. Strozier, *Self Psychology and the Humanities: Reflections on a New Psychoanalytic Approach* (New York: W.W. Norton, 1985).

False forms of listening

Sometimes what appears to be listening is not really listening at all. Below is a list of some relatively common forms of false listening.[24] These give the young person the impression that we are being present to them even when we are not, at least not fully. In the end, these lead to growing miscommunication and frustration. We highlight these false forms of listening because some of them may be easy to fall into without growing self-awareness and integrity.

Pseudo Listening: Pseudo listening refers to the misleading act of appearing to listen attentively, while actually not fully engaging with the speaker's message. When someone pseudo listens, they may give the impression of listening by nodding, maintaining eye contact, or making other nonverbal acknowledgments, but in reality, they are not paying attention to the information being shared.

Selective Listening: In selective listening, the listener focuses only on the information that they deem relevant or important to their own interests or needs. Selective listening, which may or may not be conscious, often occurs when the listener has an agenda or bias. For example, suppose you ask a young person to take up a ministry leadership position. They give you five reasons why they should not accept it and one reason why they might, but you only hear the one positive reason and you tell others that the person seems very interested.

Insulated Listening: An insulated listener actively avoids or ignores certain topics. This can occur for a variety of reasons, such as discomfort with the

---

[24] Department of Communication, Indiana State University, "5.5: Stages of Listening," in *Introduction to Public Communication* (Terre Haute, IN: Indiana State University, 2016), http://kell.indstate.edu/public-comm-intro/chapter/5-5-stages-of-listening/.

topic, fear of confrontation, or a desire to avoid unpleasant emotions. For example, a listener who is afraid of conflict may steer the conversation away from the young person's ever talking about their ongoing unethical behavior. The listener subconsciously feels, "I'd rather not know." Avoidance also occurs if the listener is uncomfortable with a certain topic because of their own lack of integration and peace about it, such as with sexuality, mortality, money, etc., or if they feel hypocritical or incompetent with regards to it. The young person will sense the listener's avoidance and intuitively avoid talking about these important topics as well.

Defensive Listening: A defensive listener perceives comments or feedback as personal attacks, leading to a defensive posture and response. Such a listener is usually feeling insecure and perceives criticism or feedback as a threat to their self-esteem. Because insecurity can powerfully distort our perception of what the young person is trying to tell us, it is important to be self-aware, to regularly ask clarifying questions, and to reflect back what we think they are saying to us. Additionally, we can work to develop a growth mindset, in which we view feedback and criticism as opportunities for growth and improvement rather than as personal attacks.

Stage Hogging: Stage hogging, also known as monopolizing, is a type of listening behavior where the listener is more focused on expressing their own ideas or interests than on understanding the speaker's perspective. The listener may interrupt the speaker, finish their sentences, or steer the conversation towards their own agenda. Listeners who engage in stage hogging often have a strong need to be the center of attention and frequently engage in mental rehearsal. They may also use verbal cues such as "yeah, but" or "I know how you feel" to shift the conversation back to themselves. This type of false listening will leave young people feeling unheard and frustrated over time.

Ambushing: Ambushing is a type of listening behavior where the listener carefully and attentively gathers information with the intention of using it as an attack against the other person. The listener may even ask questions designed to trap the speaker. An ambushing mentality makes it impossible to genuinely understand the young person's perspective, which is a necessary step to good communication, even if one disagrees with it.

| Pseudolistening | Selective | Insulated | Defensive | Stage Hogging | Ambushing |

Key Points:

1. There are many barriers to discriminative, content-oriented, and relational listening. Knowing these barriers and growing in self-awareness about them can help us improve.

2. Discriminative listening can be hindered by physiological, cognitive, and environmental barriers.

3. Content-oriented listening can be hindered by trying to control the narrative, superficial distractions, intellectual insecurity, mental disorganization, and closeness-communication bias.

4. Relational listening can be hindered by objectivity-bias, affective insecurity, emotional projection, person-idea conflation, extraordinary expectations, and mental rehearsal.

5. False forms of listening include pseudo listening, selective listening, insulated listening, defensive listening, stage-hogging, and ambushing.

Reflection Questions:

1. What improvements can you make to your environment to remove listening barriers?
2. Which content-oriented barriers do you notice in your behaviors or mindset?
3. Which relational barriers do you notice in your behaviors or mindset?
4. Do you ever engage in any of the false forms of listening? If so, what would help you avoid them going forward?

CHAPTER 7

Skills and Limits

Mindset, environment, and posture

Listening is an art and a skill. To become better listeners, we must have the right *mindset* or attitude towards listening. Listening should be considered a dynamic and engaging process, rather than a passive activity. We should desire to listen with an open and unbiased mind, a nonjudgmental attitude, and an abundance of empathy. A true listening mindset is one that is ready to give ample time for young people to express themselves, allowing them even to stumble around and say wrong things along the process of developing trust and finding their voice. We learn to approach conversations with genuine *curiosity* and a sense of *wonder*. A healthy curiosity about the young person's thoughts, desires, perspectives, and background will help us stay engaged and other-centered. Likewise, an interior sense of wonder will yield sensitivity to the transcendent value of the image of God who is before us and who always remains a wonderful mystery. Wonder will fill us with reverence, gratitude, gentleness, and love in our interactions with young people.

Alongside the right mindset, the right *environment* for listening will help avoid some of the barriers mentioned in the previous chapter. Even if ambiance is not important to some listeners, we should not assume the same for those that we are listening to. A peaceful, aesthetically pleasing environment goes a long way towards making a person feel comfortable. If your meeting space is in your office, have a few chairs situated away from your desk so that the young person does not feel like they are one of the items on your to-do list. If it is possible to have more than two chairs, the person will feel free to sit where they feel comfortable in relation to you. Relatively lighter chairs are also helpful because the person can make slight adjustments to their angle and distance. Two chairs that face each

other convey a strong sense of intentionality, connection, and focus. The speaker may or may not be comfortable with this setup. If this is uncomfortable, sitting at a slight angle can create a more relaxed or casual atmosphere by alleviating the pressure of constant eye contact, allowing the person to turn towards you whenever they want.

Many sources suggest that certain *postures* are better than others for showing interest and openness. It is difficult to determine which of these claims have proven effects and in which circumstances. Dr. Peter Bull, an expert in the microanalysis of nonverbal communication,[1] conducted a series of well-controlled experiments to test popular hypotheses with granular precision.[2] The participants in his experiments were not role-playing. In fact, they were not even aware that their posture was being studied, making their responses particularly genuine. The first set of experiments determined which postures expressed (encoded) interest, boredom, agreement, or disagreement. The second set of experiments determined how various postures were perceived (decoded) by another person.

---

[1] "Peter Bull - Psychology, University of York," accessed July 19, 2023, https://www.york.ac.uk/psychology/staff/honoraryandassociates/peb1/.

[2] P. E. Bull, *Posture & Gesture*, International Series in Experimental Social Psychology 16 (Pergamon, 1987).

For our purposes, we are more interested in the decoding of posture because we want to know how the young person perceives me when I am listening in a particular posture. Based on these two sets of experiments, we offer the following recommendations for listening posture.

1. Folded arms: Folded arms consistently encode *disagreement* and are decoded as *disagreement* by the person you are listening to. This is one of the most decisive conclusions of the study.
    → *Recommendation*: Avoid folded arms.

2. Leaning in: You tend to lean in when you feel *interested* and lean back when you feel bored. Most people will perceive (decode) these actions along the same lines. However, there are nuances. If your legs are stretched out or you support your head with your hand while you are leaning in, the person will decode boredom.[3]
    → *Recommendation*: Slightly leaning in towards the person with legs drawn back and hands on the abdomen is a posture that communicates well.

3. Crossed legs: Contrary to popular belief, crossed legs are decoded more positively than uncrossed legs. Crossing above the bottom knee is perceived as more *friendly and relaxed*. Crossed legs that cover the bottom knee can be perceived as *polite*.[4]
    → *Recommendation*: Cross your legs as you feel comfortable (except in settings where this would be considered irreverent).

4. Straight vs sideways lean: A straight head posture is usually perceived as *interested*, whereas the head leaning to the side is perceived as *relaxed*. A straight body posture is perceived as *polite*,

---

[3] Bull, tbl. 7.
[4] Bull, 81-82.

while the body leaning to the side is perceived as *relaxed.*[5]

→ *Recommendation*: <u>Feel free to lean your head or body to the side during relaxed portions of the conversation.</u>

5. Supporting head with hand: Supporting your head with your hand can be decoded as *boredom*. There are exceptions, such as when you are sitting straight or leaning to the side.[6] But when you lean forward while supporting your head, it looks like you are practically asleep, with your hand being the only thing keeping your head from falling.

    → *Recommendation*: <u>You may support your head if you are sitting straight or leaning to the side, in a way that communicates a comfortable, attentive, or inquisitive disposition of listening. Be sure not to communicate boredom.</u>

LISTENING POSTURE
Checklist

- ✓ Avoid folded arms.

- ✓ Slightly leaning in towards the person with legs drawn back and hands on the abdomen is a posture that communicates well.

- ✓ Cross your legs as you feel comfortable (except in settings where this would be considered irreverent)

- ✓ Feel free to lean your head or body to the side during relaxed portions of the conversation.

- ✓ You may support your head if you are sitting straight or leaning to the side, in a way that communicates a comfortable, attentive, or inquisitive disposition of listening. Be sure not to communicate boredom.

---

[5] Ibid.

[6] Bull, tbl. 7.

The listening dialogue

Effective listeners do not just wait for opportunities to listen. Through their verbal and nonverbal invitations, they make others feel comfortable opening up. Listening is in fact a form of dialogue, which often begins with a *prompt* from the listener. After the prompt, the majority of time is given to the young person who is speaking, but the listener must stay engaged and *communicate engagement* throughout the listening process. If the young person were not looking for the active reception of their message, they would simply speak to an object or pet instead.

The listening dialogue begins with *open questions*, which prompt the speaker to provide more detailed and thoughtful responses than simply "yes" or "no".[7] By using open questions, you encourage the speaker to elaborate on their thoughts, feelings, or experiences, and this helps foster a deeper interaction.

Closed Question Example:

"Do you think that you would enjoy a career in engineering?"

Open Question Example:

"What do you find attractive about a possible career in engineering?"

Asking the right type of question may seem like a nifty technique. Any closed question can be refashioned into an open question. For example, "Did you like your new job?" could be rephrased as "How does it feel

---

[7] William Miller and Stephen Rollnick, *Motivational Interviewing: Helping People Change*, 3rd ed (New York: The Guilford Press, 2012).

working at your new job?" Or, if we already asked a closed question, we can follow-up with a question that opens it up: "I see. What do you like about it?" So far, this is at the level of a technique. It is more important, however, to examine whether our way of being with and prompting young people in conversation *opens them up to greater self-discovery and self-revelation*. Our questions should help them express their dreams, interior conflicts, unarticulated fears, joys, etc. If these never come up in our regular conversations with young people, our way of engaging them is not yet sufficiently open. There are many dimensions along which open questions could be asked. Some will help clarify emotion, such as "What are you feeling right now?" and further "Could you describe that feeling a little more?" Asking for a list of answers can help a person search within, even if they are not used to providing in-depth responses. For example, "What are five talents that the Lord has blessed you with for the good of the Church or world?" Other questions explore hypothetical situations or states, such as, "If you had no fear at all, what would you do about this situation?" In like manner, there are innumerable open questions that can be asked to help young people open up.

Asking grammatically closed (yes/no) but *conceptually open questions* can be a powerful tool to elicit greater clarity and depth of thought.[8] Doing so can bring subconscious tensions to the surface. For example, "Is this job everything you had hoped it would be?" is technically a yes/no question, but, for a person who is wrestling with that very question, it cannot be answered without reflection and nuanced explanation. The person will hopefully come to greater clarity and peace just by talking through it. Asking a thoughtful seminarian, "Can you imagine yourself as a priest?",

---

[8] Peter Worley, "Open Thinking, Closed Questioning: Two Kinds of Open and Closed Question," *Journal of Philosophy in Schools* 2, no. 2 (November 30, 2015), https://doi.org/10.21913/JPS.v2i2.1269.

will often evoke a deep response because of the amount of time and prayer and feeling that has already gone into this question.

After asking open questions, verbal and nonverbal *acknowledgments* such as "mhmm..", "I see..", "Oh no..", and head nods provide the young person with simple reassurances that you are following along with them. A poker-faced listener can make a young person who is trying to be vulnerable very nervous and so incapable of truly opening up. In difficult conversations, ordinary and sincere acknowledgments also convey that there are no off-limit topics and that the listener renders no condemnation or rejection. Acknowledgments convey the patience to hear the whole story and to gain a full understanding before opining (as in analytical listening). Respect is a fundamental aspect of effective listening, and it involves acknowledging and valuing the young person's opinions, even when they differ from one's own.

Affirmation is the practice and attitude of seeking out and appreciating the young person's strengths and efforts. It is the opposite of an *evaluative mentality* that always seeks out what is wrong with the person in order to fix it.[9] It is never easy for a person to see their own graced capacity to overcome major challenges. Everyone needs encouragement from others. As a listener, you can help a young person pause to acknowledge their own positive efforts, to celebrate their small wins, to remember their past successes, and to focus on their strengths. In difficult situations, even the act of speaking to you may be a feat of courage that should be affirmed.

Affirmation is a fine balance because you do not want the person to become dependent on your validation. For this reason, affirmation should not be an answer to the implicit question, "Do you think I'm doing well?" Young people will often seek this out. They may desire for someone to take away the weight of responsibility from their choices by telling them if their

---

[9] Miller and Rollnick, 19.

choices are right or wrong. Answering this question (in any of its many forms) will make you an arbiter of good and bad and the one who defines the standards of success and failure, which would of course be highly problematic. Carl Rogers wrote, "Curiously enough a positive evaluation is as threatening in the long run as a negative one, since to inform someone that he is good implies that you also have the right to tell him he is bad."[10] True affirmation does not offer this but simply provides the encouragement the person needs to keep going and to keep growing.

Affirmation Examples:

1) *"I appreciate your courage in sharing this with me."*
2) *"You've been through a lot in your life, but you've always managed to hang in there with incredible faith and trust."*
3) *"You can get through this with the Lord, and you will come out even stronger."*

Empathy is a central aspect of effective listening, particularly in relational listening contexts. While the inner experience of empathy is the most important, *expressing empathy* is also necessary. The measure of your skill is simply how much a young person feels empathized with when they speak to you. If they sense that you feel what they are going through, they will open up more. They will describe not just external events, but their inner experience. You will help them relish good experiences more and process negative ones.

---

[10] Carl R. Rogers, *On Becoming a Person* (New York: Houghton Mifflin Harcourt, 1961), 55.

Expressing Empathy Examples:

1) *"My goodness, this is such great news!"*
2) *"That must be heartbreaking, losing such a close friend so unexpectedly."*

Reflecting is the act of paraphrasing or summarizing the speaker's words to regularly confirm understanding and demonstrate active engagement. Carl Rogers named this "active empathy," and his student Thomas Gordon coined the term *active listening* for it.[11] The goal is to reflect back the essence of what the speaker has said by using our own words. As we do so, our interpretation and inferences will also come to light, and the person can either correct them or confirm them. Reflecting takes practice and is different from repeating because we must comprehend and re-express their message. This helps the young person feel heard and understood and helps the listener more actively engage with their thoughts and feelings. Reflecting can help protect us from projection or other forms of excessive top-down processing.

Reflecting Example:

Speaker: *"I'm really disappointed that she hasn't texted me this whole weekend. I thought we had something going. It's all I can think about, all day long."*

Listener: *"It sounds like you're questioning whether she's really interested in you and that you've been worrying about it a lot."*

---

[11] Miller and Rollnick, 48.

Once we have listened for some time, *summarizing* is a helpful practice that involves providing a concise overview of the key points or themes discussed so far. It helps to ensure mutual understanding and clarity in longer conversations or discussions, especially ones involving multiple topics. When the young person hears a summary of what they have said so far, it helps them to see an overarching view of their situation with fresh eyes. It also gives them encouragement to keep talking because they see that they are indeed making sense and progress. Sometimes, summarizing serves as a transitional movement, allowing you and the young person to bring closure to the current topic and to move the conversation forward.

Summarizing Examples:

1) *"So you're saying that you do get along with everyone in your youth group, but you also feel like no one would care if they lost your friendship. You doubt whether anyone is truly interested in you as a person. Is that right?"*

2) *"I'm eager to hear about your experience at the retreat. Before we get there, let me see if I understand the struggles you have been describing that led up to the retreat. You were really angry at your parents for treating you like a child. You tried to assert your independence by ignoring some of their rules, which made them all the more strict with you, and this became a vicious cycle. Did I get that right?"*

Occasionally, it may be helpful to *check in*, which is like stepping out of the conversation for a moment in order to see how well it is progressing. Together, you check in to see if the conversation is achieving its purpose or whether it should take a different direction or approach. Checking in is not always necessary, at least not explicitly. Often, you can pick up small indications from the young person about how they feel the conversation is going. The young person might say, "This is really helpful" or "I'm glad we're talking about this," for example. If there is anything unsaid, uncomfortableness, or awkward lingering, that would be a perfect time to check in. This shows the young person respect, as it gives them an opportunity to redirect the conversation in a way that is most helpful to them. It also gives them ownership and active participation in the conversation. If it turns out that the conversation is not going well, you could always propose a fresh start.

Check-In Examples:

1) *"How is this conversation going for you?"*
2) *"Is this conversation helping? Is there a different way you would like to approach it?"*

In certain contexts, *taking notes* will be highly beneficial, assuming the young person is comfortable with it. Taking notes helps you track the speaker's thought process more carefully because it requires you to listen attentively throughout, to process whatever is said, and to summarize it at regular intervals. Taking notes also allows you to get a very high-level view of the conversations, especially ones that span multiple meetings, which will then help you notice patterns and draw connections. Finally, it can help you recall concrete instances that demonstrate growth to affirm the young person very effectively. Of course, if note-taking seems awkward or intimidating in a given context, these factors might outweigh its benefits. You could also ask if the young person would be comfortable with you taking notes afterwards to help you serve them better. Protecting the security of digital and physical notes is always necessary.

Finally, *self-reflection* after conversations will help you improve your listening skills. Running through the key moments of the conversation and noticing where you listened well and where you could improve will give you the necessary reinforcement and help you make adjustments. The three listening types from Chapter 4 provide a framework for analyzing the skills appropriate to different listening contexts. Training programs for youth ministers, spiritual directors, formators, counselors, etc., that teach effective listening skills are always recommended. Another way to grow is by asking for feedback and receiving it with an open mind. In the end, listening is an art and a skill. Developing the skill will help you flourish in your own approach to the art of listening to young people.

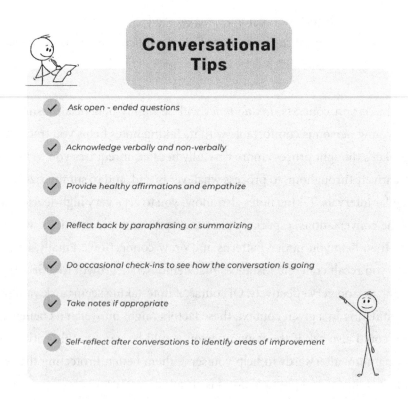

Conversational Tips

✓ Ask open - ended questions

✓ Acknowledge verbally and non-verbally

✓ Provide healthy affirmations and empathize

✓ Reflect back by paraphrasing or summarizing

✓ Do occasional check-ins to see how the conversation is going

✓ Take notes if appropriate

✓ Self-reflect after conversations to identify areas of improvement

When to stop listening

So far we have focused on maximizing one's listening potential. But there are also times to stop listening. Aristotle taught that virtue lies in the middle of two extremes.  This book has focused on remedying the widespread listening deficiency, but there is such a thing as too much listening. Usually in these situations, someone else would be better suited to help the young person.

The word trauma is used quite broadly today. Difficult interactions, ordinary grief, or other painful experiences are not the same as trauma, though the term is popularly used in these contexts today.[12] Actual trauma has physiological effects and alters our capacities to perceive, think, and feel.[13] According to the *Diagnostic and Statistical Manual of Mental Disorders*, trauma is "exposure to *actual or threatened death, serious injury, or sexual violence*," and can be experienced directly or indirectly in the following ways: *directly experiencing* traumatic events, *witnessing* traumatic events, *learning that* traumatic events occurred to someone close, or *experiencing repeated or extreme exposure to aversive details* of the traumatic events.[14] As someone working with young people, it is very likely that you

---

[12] Greg Lukianoff and Jonathan Haidt, *The Coddling of the American Mind: How Good Intentions and Bad Ideas Are Setting Up a Generation for Failure* (New York: Penguin Books, 2018), 25.

[13] Bessel van der Kolk, *The Body Keeps the Score: Brain, Mind, and Body in the Healing of Trauma* (New York: Penguin Books, 2015), 21.

[14] American Psychiatric Association, *Diagnostic and Statistical Manual of Mental Disorders*, 5th ed. (Arlington, VA: American Psychiatric Publishing, 2013), 271, emphases added.

will listen to someone opening up about their trauma at some point. If you are exposed to trauma with a high-level of detail, you may become traumatized yourself. If a young person begins to share graphic details with you about sexual molestation or domestic violence, for example, unless you are a professional, you would need to refer them to a counselor. (Depending on the case, you may be legally obliged to report it first.) Without help, you may become overwhelmed by the experience and start to exhibit signs of trauma yourself. Those with high empathy are even more likely to experience such *Secondary Traumatic Stress*, which includes intrusive and repeated replaying of the traumatic content. Even among those who are trained for dealing with trauma, secondary traumatic stress is common, affecting anywhere from 15%-39% of professionals.[15] When working with trauma survivors, therefore, it is crucially important to know our limits and to know when to stop listening. This is the only way to ensure that the young person will get the help that they need.

Strong feelings of empathy (or, more likely, projection) can make it difficult to listen to a young person's problems with healthy boundaries. There is a danger that we will gradually insert ourselves into the equation. *Over-involvement* occurs when we become one of the intermediary steps between their short-term actions. For example, you listen to a young man tell you about how his relationship with his fiancee is falling apart and you encourage him to reconcile with her. He talks to her and then immediately reaches out to you again. He needs your advice or encouragement between each step. If you find yourself frequently responding to calls and messages throughout the day or at odd hours, there is a high chance you are over-involved or are creating a *codependency*. If you are neglecting

---

[15] Roman Cieslak et al., "Secondary Trauma Self-Efficacy: Concept and Its Measurement," *Psychological Assessment* 25, no. 3 (September 2013): 917–28, https://doi.org/10.1037/a0032687.

your own prayer life, well-being, responsibilities, or relationships because of the young person's problems, these are major warning signs of over-involvement and codependency as well. You can avoid entering into a pattern of over-involvement by surrendering the issues to God and exercising *patient trust*. Have the young person schedule meetings or calls with you at least a week or two in advance, so that you are not putting out every fire. Instead of being involved in each and every step, let your conversations be about discerning the overarching trends and patterns in their life. In this way, you can avoid the danger of false responsibility and control over another person's life. Most importantly, encourage the young person to bring their challenges directly to God in prayer, to trust in Him, and to seek out His guidance and help. If you are already over-involved and/or codependent, it is important to acknowledge your limits, to step away from the relationship, and to ask someone else to support the young person.

We understand that supporting someone who is going through difficult times is essential to Christian charity. But *enabling* someone works against charity because it does harm to the other rather than good. Enabling protects a person again and again from facing the true consequences of their actions. It covers for their habitual irresponsibility, imprudence, lack of seriousness, immaturity, substance abuse, or any other dysfunctional behavior. The young person will usually be grateful and even sorry each time, but the pattern will repeat and grow worse. Each time, the enabler knows that if they do not help this "one last time" the young person will crash and burn.[16] In the case of listening, enabling often takes the form of *giving affirmations undeservedly out of a false sense of compassion.*

---

[16] Michelle Pugle, "Helping vs. Enabling: What's the Difference?," Psych Central, March 14, 2018, https://psychcentral.com/health/what-is-the-difference-between-supporting-and-enabling.

We listen to a young person making major mistakes and rather than helping them acknowledge the obvious incongruities or negative patterns, we affirm them because we do not want them to be discouraged. More and more, they become dependent on our affirmations to help them cope with life's difficulties. As each new problem arises, the stakes become higher for the enabler. A failure to affirm would now produce a seemingly catastrophic effect. When an enabler suddenly stops affirming the young person, a reaction might sound something like this: "If it was anyone else, I could take it. But from you, it is so painful. I thought you understood me and supported me." Enabling can be avoided by safeguarding our integrity from the beginning, which means to be simultaneously loving and truthful. Put another way, resolve to *never affirm behavior or choices that you believe are harmful.* As Pope Benedict XVI wrote, "Without truth, charity degenerates into sentimentality. Love becomes an empty shell, to be filled in an arbitrary way."[17] If you feel that you are too far into the enabler pattern to be able to back out constructively, it is time to find someone else that can help them more effectively.

Key Points:

1. Effective listening comes from a mindset of patient receptivity, understanding perspectives, suspending biases, seeking clarity, and feeling empathy. Most importantly, it involves a genuine curiosity and sense of wonder about the mystery of the other person.

---

[17] Pope Benedict XVI, "Caritas in Veritate," 2009, 3, https://www.vatican.va/content/benedict-xvi/en/encyclicals/documents/hf_ben-xvi_enc_20090629_caritas-in-veritate.html.

2. Creating the right environment makes a positive impact. Pay attention to the ambiance of the environment, whether it conveys task-orientedness, relaxed conversation, or more intense interpersonal communication. To be an effective listener, we should be mindful of how our posture is perceived or decoded by the listener. For example, leaning in can communicate interest and crossing our legs can communicate relaxed conversation.

3. Listening is a kind of dialogue and it often begins with asking open questions and then following the conversation with acknowledging, affirming, reflecting, expressing empathy, summarizing, checking in, and optionally taking notes. Self-reflection afterwards is encouraged for continual improvement of one's listening skills.

4. There are certain situations in which listening can become harmful, such as with secondary traumatic stress and patterns of overinvolvement, codependency, or enabling.

Reflection Questions:

1. How well do I maintain a non-judgmental attitude when listening to young people?

2. Do my words and nonverbal expressions adequately communicate the empathy that I feel? Or, if needed, how can I improve?

3. How often do I affirm young people for their efforts, sincerity, past successes, or willingness to open up? How does this compare with my evaluative tendencies?

4. Are there situations past or present when it was/is necessary to stop listening to someone?

CHAPTER 8

How Young People Want To Be Listened To

The previous chapters have examined the art of listening from the perspectives of research, clinical practice, and pastoral experience. However, we want to end this book about listening to young people by *listening to young people*. What do young people have to tell us about how they would like to be listened to? Through our various networks, we conducted a survey and received 193 responses (92 male, 65 female, 36 undisclosed) from 15-24 year olds. These responses, while they came in from seven countries, do not claim to be a perfect representation of the average views of all young people. For one, most of them are connected with the Church, though at varying levels. Secondly, 50% of the respondents are from the USA and 37% are from India. Still, their voices are important and provide both nuance and authenticity to what has been said about listening so far.

In the first few hours of its deployment, we realized that the majority of young people would not take the time to fill out a long survey. We had to trim the survey down to just ten closed-form questions and two open-ended questions. Designing the questions and then seeing the responses was reassuring and eye-opening. With some of the questions, for example, we anticipated different responses from males and females. These proved to be the case, even more than we expected. For a few questions, we assumed the results would be so obvious that we wondered whether to even include the question at all. In fact, the results turned out surprisingly diverse. For example, only 56% of respondents reported experiencing difficulty opening up to someone who points out their imperfections and failures (even less, only 52% among American respondents). We thought this would be more like 90%, but, as it turns out, men are surprisingly open to having their imperfections and failures pointed out to them. Indeed, while the overall results certainly confirm the significance of empathic listening, they also reveal a greater openness in young people to being understood and receiving guidance than is often recognized. The typology of different listening types presented in Chapter 4 becomes all the more important. The data collection phase of our survey was completed in two short weeks, from July 5, 2023 to July 19, 2023, thanks to the support of our networks and friends who distributed it far and wide. We present the findings below with gratitude to all the young people who took the time to fill out the survey, who provided thoughtful responses to the open-ended questions, and who offered to be interviewed for additional information.

1. I find it difficult to open up with people who point out my imperfections and failures.

Ashley (20 years old, Texas)[1]: Yeah, I think being non-judgemental is im-

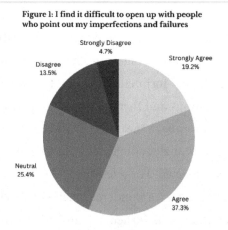

Figure 1: I find it difficult to open up with people who point out my imperfections and failures

Strongly Disagree 4.7%
Disagree 13.5%
Strongly Agree 19.2%
Neutral 25.4%
Agree 37.3%

portant. I think that's a major thing. Even if the person doesn't have much advice or anything, just being open to listening and listening in a non-judgmental way is important. ...Whatever it is, do not judge. And just helping them but never accusing, never grouping them, having no preconception of who they are before approaching them. And just being very open to just listening to whatever they have to say.

---

[1] Names have been replaced to preserve anonymity.

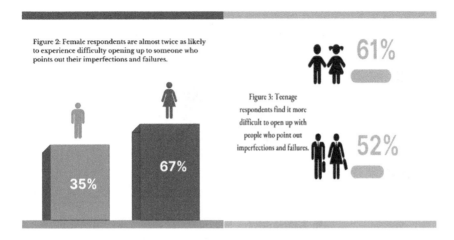

Figure 2: Female respondents are almost twice as likely to experience difficulty opening up to someone who points out their imperfections and failures.

61%

Figure 3: Teenage respondents find it more difficult to open up with people who point out imperfections and failures.

52%

67%

35%

2. **I cannot engage in a deeper conversation with someone who frequently offers their opinion about what I'm saying.**

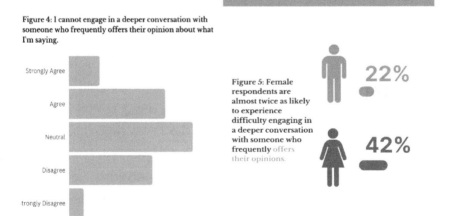

Figure 4: I cannot engage in a deeper conversation with someone who frequently offers their opinion about what I'm saying.

Strongly Agree

Agree

Neutral

Disagree

trongly Disagree

0   10   20   30   40

Figure 5: Female respondents are almost twice as likely to experience difficulty engaging in a deeper conversation with someone who frequently offers their opinions.

22%

42%

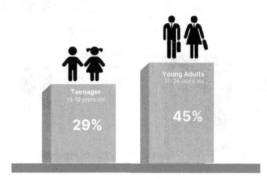

Figure 6: Young adult respondents find it more difficult to engage in a deeper conversation with someone who frequently offers their opinions.

3. I can be more open with people who make eye contact when I'm talking to them.

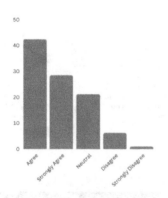

Figure 7: I can be more open with people who make eye contact when I'm talking to them.

71% of the participants concurred (agreed or strongly agreed) that they feel more open and comfortable when engaging with individuals who make eye contact during conversations. Eye contact is a powerful non-verbal cue that fosters trust, connection, and understanding between speakers and listeners. When listeners maintain eye contact, young people feel genuinely heard and valued, leading to increased willingness to share their thoughts, feelings, and personal experiences.

4. I am not able to express myself when someone interrupts my flow.

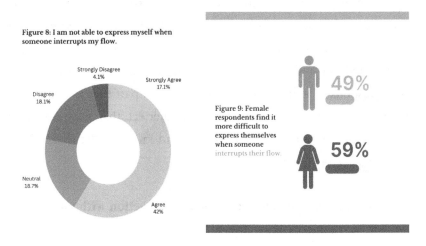

Figure 8: I am not able to express myself when someone interrupts my flow.

Strongly Disagree 4.1%

Strongly Agree 17.1%

Disagree 18.1%

Neutral 18.7%

Agree 42%

Figure 9: Female respondents find it more difficult to express themselves when someone interrupts their flow.

49%

59%

59% of the participants find it challenging to express themselves when someone interrupts their flow during conversations. This highlights the importance of active listening and respectful communication, where uninterrupted exchanges foster greater self-expression. This does not mean that one cannot offer one's opinion or that there should not be any back and forth. As seen above, most participants do not mind if a listener frequently offers their opinions (especially men). Even when offering one's opinions or thoughts, however, this should be done artfully, so as not to interrupt a person's flow.

Susan (18 years old, Florida): If I'm trying to say something, especially to my parents, when they don't listen to the full thing, as soon as I say, like, 2% of what I was trying to say, they're like, "No, no," or they say something so quickly and I'm like, "Oh. I wasn't even done talking." So, yeah, just reacting so quickly. And then, that's going to make me not want to keep talking...

Helen (23 years old, Illinois): I would say for me, one quality I expect [is someone] not interjecting too much, not interrupting too much. Just on the exterior.. at the very first level, don't talk when you're trying to listen. Yeah, first, when someone can kind of just absorb [what] I'm saying, and they're nodding and maybe they're saying like, "mmm..", or they're giving some responsive affirmation, but for the most part they're not trying to interrupt what I'm saying, not trying to interject, that always makes me more comfortable to continue sharing and knowing that I could share with this person again.

---

5.   **I tend to shut off when I am given instruction without my asking for it.**

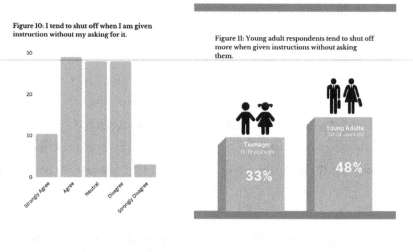

Figure 10: I tend to shut off when I am given instruction without my asking for it.

Figure 11: Young adult respondents tend to shut off more when given instructions without asking them.

6. I inquire about the credibility of a person with my peers before opening up to someone relatively new

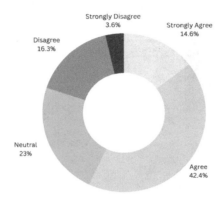

Figure 12: I inquire about the credibility of a person with my peers before opening up to someone relatively new

For more than half of the respondents (57%), credibility matters. They will not open up to someone without first knowing that they can be trusted.

7. I expect practical guidance for my issues when I choose to speak about them with others.

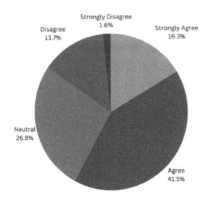

Figure 13: I expect practical guidance for my issues when I choose to speak about them with others.

8.   I expect empathy when I choose to speak about my issues with others.

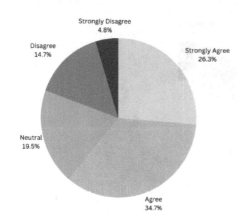

Figure 14: I expect empathy when I choose to speak about my issues with others.

61% of respondents look for empathy in a listener and 58% look for practical guidance. Both of these are clearly essential. At the same time, there are important differences along gender lines, as indicated in figures 15(a) and 15(b).

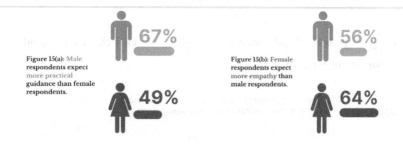

Figure 15(a): Male respondents expect more practical guidance than female respondents.

Figure 15(b): Female respondents expect more empathy than male respondents.

9. Having someone listen to me was one of the important factors of my success.

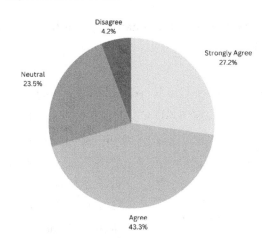

Figure 16: Having someone listen to me was one of the important factors of my success.

71% of respondents agree or strongly agree that having someone genuinely listen to them played an important role in their success, perhaps their personal, spiritual, or early academic and professional success. In other words, **young people recognize the immense value of listeners**. Considering the fact that many young people may not have even experienced attentive listening before, at least to the full extent described in this book, the fact that nearly 7 out of 10 of our respondents have already seen its impact in their lives speaks volumes. Perhaps not surprisingly, 86% of those who agreed with this statement, also agreed with the next survey prompt, which is about looking for maturity, wisdom, and understanding in someone before opening up to them. When the right person stands ready to listen, it makes all the difference.

Ashley (20 years old, Texas): I think the major thing is that when you're able to talk to someone, it really removes whatever burden you're holding. So it helps you, you know? Sometimes when you think about whatever burden you're having, when you think it's too much.. when you're able to talk to someone, you can actually kind of handle it better. Maybe you're thinking about it too much and it's not as big as you feel it is.. having someone listen to you just helps you handle whatever you're going through.

---

10. I look for maturity, wisdom, and understanding in others before being vulnerable with them.

A striking **83%** of young people look for these qualities before being vulnerable with someone. 90% of those who indicated that they inquire first into the credibility of a listener (see figure 12) also agreed with this statement. Maturity, wisdom, and understanding are clearly among the most important characteristics that make someone a credible listener. In fact, as represented in the next survey question, *understanding* is the single most important quality for our respondents.

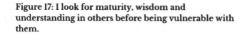

Figure 17: I look for maturity, wisdom and understanding in others before being vulnerable with them.

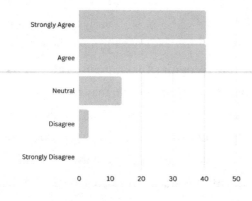

Paul (18 years old, Texas): The experience that older people have is something that can only be gained through time. I myself have a lot of older people that I talk to. And yeah, their perspective on a situation means a lot because, especially if it's someone that's maybe like 12 years older than you, they understand what you're going through and they can help, not steer, but show you the right way, which is something that you won't get from peers as much, as we're friends.

11. List the top 3 qualities that make you feel comfortable opening up to someone.

Understanding

Trustworthy

Humor

Patient

Non-judgmental

Empathic

Attentive

CONCLUSION

Listening makes a difference. Listening to a young person could very well change their life, as it did Victor's life from the opening chapter. Young people desire empathic and understanding listeners who are also capable of providing sound guidance when appropriate. On our part, we should be eager to fulfill this very need since it flows from our desire to love in the way that Christ loves. Each of us has different gifts. Different aspects of listening will shine more brightly in one person than another, but all of us can be more intentional about giving our time and attention to young people and about growing in our capacity as genuine listeners. Our hope is that with the research and pastoral insights from this book, assisted by grace, we can lovingly accompany the young people around us most effectively on their path to holiness by giving ourselves generously to the art of listening.

APPENDIX

Personal Listening Style Profile[1]

Below are several items that people use to describe themselves as a listener. Assess how each statement applies to you by marking your level of agreement/disagreement with each item. Please do not think of any specific listening situation but of your general ways of listening, how you typically listen in most situations.

	Strongly Disagree	Disagree	Somewhat Disagree	Unsure	Somewhat agree	Agree	Strongly Agree
1. When listening to others, I focus on any inconsistencies and/or errors in what's being said.	1	2	3	4	5	6	7
2. When listening to others, I am mainly concerned with how they are feeling.	1	2	3	4	5	6	7
3. I tend to withhold judgment about another's ideas until I have heard everything they have to say.	1	2	3	4	5	6	7
4. I get frustrated when people get off topic during a conversation.	1	2	3	4	5	6	7
5. I often catch errors in other speakers' logic.	1	2	3	4	5	6	7

---

[1] Personal Listening Style Survey - © 2015, Bodie Consulting, LLC. Based on: Bodie, G. D., Worthington, D. L., & Gearhart, C. G. (2013). The Revised Listening Styles Profile (LSP-R): Development and validation. *Communication Quarterly*, 61, 72-90. Used with permission.

6. When listening to others, I consider all sides of the issue before responding.	1	2	3	4	5	6	7
7. I enjoy listening to others because it allows me to connect with them.	1	2	3	4	5	6	7
8. I fully listen to what a person has to say before forming any opinions.	1	2	3	4	5	6	7
9. I prefer speakers who quickly get to the point.	1	2	3	4	5	6	7
10. When listening to others, I notice contradictions in what they say.	1	2	3	4	5	6	7
11. When listening to others, I focus on understanding the feelings behind words.	1	2	3	4	5	6	7
12. I find it difficult to listen to people who take too long to get their ideas across.	1	2	3	4	5	6	7

Scoring the survey: This survey identifies your personal listening style.

- Relational Listening Style Score:
  Sum your responses to Items 2, 7, 11. _____
- Analytical Listening Style Score:
  Sum your responses to Items 3, 6, 8. _____
- Task-Oriented Score:
  Sum your responses to Items 4, 9, 12. _____
- Critical Listening Style Score:
  Sum your answers to Items 1, 5, 10. _____

The style for which you have the highest sum is your preferred personal listening style. Some people have one dominant style, while others will have two with close scores. A few people do not have a dominant style and can switch listening modes as needed.

HOW TO INTERPRET AND USE YOUR SCORE

The "styles" you calculated above represent four distinct goals that listeners have when engaged in situations that call them to be a particular kind of listener.

The first listening-related goal is labeled **relational listening** (RL), which describes a concern with and awareness of others' feelings and emotions.

When listening relationally,

- people are viewed as more empathic, and
- their speech is likely more relationally oriented.

In addition, people who report listening in this way also report being more outgoing and sociable.

So when you listen to your romantic partner talk about how stressful it was at work today or you try to understand how your co-worker feels about a recent medical diagnosis, you should focus your listening energies on their feelings and emotions, trying to connect and build the relationship.

The second goal, **analytical listening** (AL), reflects an orientation toward attending to the full message of a speaker before coming to judgment. Items such as "I fully listen to what a person has to say before forming any opinions," recognize a listener's desire to gather all available information with the intention of truly understanding all available perspectives.

This listening goal is likely to enable the listener to better view an issue from another person's perspective.

When listeners are primarily interested in speakers "getting to the point," they are engaged in task-oriented listening (TOL), which generally causes feelings of frustration in the listener.

- This frustration is usually manifest in a dislike for speakers who take too long to get their point across.

- Listening in a task-oriented way reflects concern with the amount of time spent in an interaction, but also represents a desire by the listener for a speaker to stay focused and on-topic.

If you can recall a time when you felt rushed listening and became frustrated when someone seemed to be "wasting your time," you likely had this goal driving your listening.

Finally, **critical listening** (CL) refers to a tendency to focus attention on the accuracy and consistency of a speaker's message. The items that measure CL tap a tendency to evaluate and critically assess messages. Basically, this goal might reflect individual needs to critically examine people and information in general.

If you have ever used listening to uncover inconsistencies in, for instance, the presentation of a politician or even a friend who seems to be "all over the place" while arguing for an issue, you have likely had the critical listening goal in mind.

And you might even be encouraged to use this type of listening in your career, like when a customer presents conflicting information or beliefs. This sort of "critically thinking" about what a customer says are his or her wants and needs turn into "critically listening" when you approach these inconsistencies with a mind toward reconciling them.

Listening is goal directed, meaning that even if you are unaware you are listening for the who, what, when, and where. Your listening changes as a function of the situation, and you should remain mindful of how this generally occurs. Practice trying to recognize elements of complex situations that correspond for a particular type of listening.

For the most part situations are complex, calling for the employment of multiple listening goals. Customers need to be listened to relationally and their views analytically, but you have a task to complete. Sometimes customers present contradictory information, and you job is to pick up on those clues; BUT you should wait until the opportune time to use that information. Be strategic in your listening. Don't interrupt just to make a point. Ask questions to get to the heart of an issue. After the person has told his or her whole story, then you can bring up past information – paraphrase their needs and gently make them realize that they may have expressed competing claims.

So that you can begin to assess the appropriateness of each listening goal, complete the following:

For each listening goal, construct a scenario that reflects appropriate use.

Relational Listening

_____

_____

_____

Analytical Listening

_____

_____

_____

Task-Oriented Listening

_____

_____

_____

Critical Listening

_____

_____

_____

BIBLIOGRAPHY

Abrahams, Robin, and Boris Groysberg. "How to Become a Better Listener." *Harvard Business Review*, December 21, 2021. https://hbr.org/2021/12/how-to-become-a-better-listener.

Adams, Richard E., Joseph A. Boscarino, and Charles R. Figley. "Compassion Fatigue and Psychological Distress among Social Workers: A Validation Study." *American Journal of Orthopsychiatry* 76, no. 1 (2006): 103–8. https://doi.org/10.1037/0002-9432.76.1.103.

Allers, Rudolph. "St. Augustine's Doctrine on Illumination." *Franciscan Studies* 12, no. 1 (1952): 27–46.

Anderson, Monica. "Teens, Social Media and Technology 2018." *Pew Research Center: Internet, Science & Tech* (blog), May 31, 2018. https://www.pewresearch.org/internet/2018/05/31/teens-social-media-technology-2018/.

Aquinas, Thomas. *Summa Theologica*. Edited by The Aquinas Institute. Translated by Lawrence Shapcote, 1268. www.aquinas.cc.

Arnold, W.E. "Listening: A Conceptualization." Indianapolis, IN, 1990.

ASHA. "Central Auditory Processing Disorder." American Speech-Language-Hearing Association. American Speech-Language-Hearing Association, June 16, 2023. https://www.asha.org/practice-portal/clinical-topics/central-auditory-processing-disorder/.

Association, American Psychiatric. *Diagnostic and Statistical Manual of Mental Disorders*. 5th ed. Arlington, VA: American Psychiatric Publishing, 2013.

Atkison, Paul R. "Advantages of the Socratic Method for Medical Teaching." *CMAJ* 193, no. 43 (November 1, 2021): E1665–E1665. https://doi.org/10.1503/cmaj.80194.

Augustine, and John E. Rotelle. *The Works of Saint Augustine: A Translation for the 21st Century*. 2nd ed. Hyde Park, N.Y.: New City Press,

2012.

Augustinus, Aurelius, and Maria Boulding. *The Works of Saint Augustine. Vol.1:Pt.1. Books The Confessions / Introduction, Translation and Notes: Maria Boulding*. 9. print., 1. pocket-size Ed. Vol. 1. Hyde Park, NY: New City Pr, 2013.

Baese-Berk, Melissa M., Drew J. McLaughlin, and Kevin B. McGowan. "Perception of Non-Native Speech." *Language and Linguistics Compass* 14, no. 7 (2020): e12375. https://doi.org/10.1111/lnc3.12375.

Bender, I. E., and A. H. Hastorf. "On Measuring Generalized Empathic Ability (Social Sensitivity)." *The Journal of Abnormal and Social Psychology* 48, no. 4 (1953): 503–6. https://doi.org/10.1037/h0054486.

Benedict XVI, Pope. "Caritas in Veritate," 2009. https://www.vatican.va/content/benedict-xvi/en/encyclicals/documents/hf_ben-xvi_enc_20090629_caritas-in-veritate.html.

———. *Jesus of Nazareth*. 1st ed. in the U.S. New York: Doubleday, 2007.

———. *Spe Salvi*, 2023. https://www.vatican.va/content/benedict-xvi/en/encyclicals/documents/hf_ben-xvi_enc_20071130_spe-salvi.html.

———. *The Nature and Mission of Theology: Essays to Orient Theology in Today's Debates*. San Francisco: Ignatius Press, 1995.

Bethune, Sophie. "Gen Z More Likely to Report Mental Health Concerns." *Monitor on Psychology* 50, no. 1 (January 2019). https://www.apa.org/monitor/2019/01/gen-z.

Bodie, Graham. "Listening as Positive Communication." In *The Positive Side of Interpersonal Communication*, edited by T. Socha and Pitts, 109–25. Peter Lang, 2012.

Bodie, Graham D., and Debra L. Worthington. "Listening Styles Profile-Revised (LSP-R)." In *The Sourcebook of Listening Research*, 402–9. John Wiley & Sons, Ltd, 2017. https://doi.org/10.1002/97811191-02991.ch42.

Bodie, Graham D., Debra L. Worthington, and Christopher C. Gearhart.

"The Listening Styles Profile-Revised (LSP-R): A Scale Revision and Evidence for Validity." *Communication Quarterly* 61, no. 1 (January 1, 2013): 72–90. https://doi.org/10.1080/01463373.2012.720343.

Bonhoeffer, Dietrich. *Life Together: The Classic Exploration of Christian in Community*. 1st edition. HarperOne, 1978.

Borghini, Giulia, and Valerie Hazan. "Listening Effort During Sentence Processing Is Increased for Non-Native Listeners: A Pupillometry Study." *Frontiers in Neuroscience* 12 (March 13, 2018): 152. https://doi.org/10.3389/fnins.2018.00152.

Bottaro, Gregory. *The Mindful Catholic: Finding God One Moment at a Time*. North Palm Beach, Florida: Beacon Publishing, 2018.

Bradbury, Rurick. "The Digital Lives of Millenials and Gen Z." May 20, 2023. https://liveperson.docsend.com/view/tm8j45m.

Bull, P. E. *Posture & Gesture*. International Series in Experimental Social Psychology 16. Pergamon, 1987.

Burgoon, Judee K., Valerie Manusov, and Laura K. Guerrero. *Nonverbal Communication*. New York: Routledge, 2016.

Cacioppo, John T., and Richard E. Petty. "The Need for Cognition." *Journal of Personality and Social Psychology* 42, no. 1 (1982): 116–31. https://doi.org/10.1037/0022-3514.42.1.116.

Camus, Albert, and Matthew Ward. *The Stranger*. 1st Vintage International ed. New York: Vintage International, 1989.

Carl R. Rogers. *On Becoming a Person*. New York: Houghton Mifflin Harcourt, 1961.

Catholic Psychotherapy Association. "Catholic Psychotherapy Assoc. - Pierced By Beauty: The Art of Healing Through Contemplative Listening," April 28, 2022. https://catholicpsychotherapy.org/event-4557255.

Center for Disease Control and Prevention. "Youth Risk Behavior Survey Data Summary & Trends Report: 2009-2019." Center for Disease

Control and Prevention, 2009. https://www.cdc.gov/healthyyouth/data/yrbs/pdf/YRBSDataSummaryTrendsReport2019-508.pdf.

Christakis, Erika. "The Dangers of Distracted Parenting." *The Atlantic*, June 16, 2018. https://www.theatlantic.com/magazine/archive/2018/07/the-dangers-of-distracted-parenting/561752/.

Cieslak, Roman, Kotaro Shoji, Aleksandra Luszczynska, Sandra Taylor, Anna Rogala, and Charles C. Benight. "Secondary Trauma Self-Efficacy: Concept and Its Measurement." *Psychological Assessment* 25, no. 3 (September 2013): 917–28. https://doi.org/10.1037/a0032687.

Coe, Erica, Jenny Cordina, Kana Enomoto, Raelyn Jacobson, Sharon Mei, and Nikhil Seshan. "Addressing Gen Z Mental Health Challenges | McKinsey." Mckinsey, January 14, 2022. https://www.mckinsey.com/industries/healthcare/our-insights/addressing-the-unprecedented-behavioral-health-challenges-facing-generation-z.

Coe, Erica, Andrew Doy, Kana Enomoto, and Cheryl Healy. "Gen Z Mental Health: The Impact of Tech and Social Media | McKinsey." Mckinsey Health Institute, May 20, 2023. https://www.mckinsey.com/mhi/our-insights/gen-z-mental-health-the-impact-of-tech-and-social-media.

Collison, Tommy, and Sunny Hong. "Does Technology Stop Us From Listening?" *Washington Square News* (blog), September 28, 2015. https://nyunews.com/2015/09/28/09-28-ops-hong/.

Coplan, Amy. "Will the Real Empathy Please Stand up? A Case for a Narrow Conceptualization." *The Southern Journal of Philosophy* 49, no. s1 (2011): 40–65. https://doi.org/10.1111/j.2041-6962.2011.00056.x.

Covey, Stephen R. *The 7 Habits of Highly Effective People*. Electronic Edition. New York: RosettaBooks, 2009.

Cowden, Richard C. "Empathy or Projection?" *Journal of Clinical Psychology* 11 (1955): 188–90. https://doi.org/10.1002/1097-4679(195504)11:2<188::AID-JCLP2270110218>3.0.CO;2-K.

Crenshaw, Dan. *Fortitude: American Resilience in the Era of Outrage*. New York: Twelve, 2020.

Curtin, Sally C. "State Suicide Rates among Adolescents and Young Adults Aged 10–24 : United States, 2000–2018." Edited by National Center for Health Statistics (U.S.). Division of Vital Statistics., National vital statistics reports ; v. 69, no. 11, 69, no. 11 (September 11, 2020). https://stacks.cdc.gov/view/cdc/93667.

Deal, Jennifer J., David G. Altman, and Steven G. Rogelberg. "Millennials at Work: What We Know and What We Need to Do (If Anything)." *Journal of Business and Psychology* 25, no. 2 (June 1, 2010): 191–99. https://doi.org/10.1007/s10869-010-9177-2.

Deloitte. "The Deloitte Global 2022 Gen Z and Millennial Survey | Deloitte Global," May 14, 2023. https://www.deloitte.com/global/en/issues/work/genzmillennialsurvey.html.

Department of Communication, Indiana State University. "5.5: Stages of Listening." In *Introduction to Public Communication*. Terre Haute, IN: Indiana State University, 2016. http://kell.indstate.edu/public-comm-intro/chapter/5-5-stages-of-listening/.

Dimock, Michael. "Defining Generations: Where Millennials End and Generation Z Begins." *Pew Research Center* (blog), January 17, 2019. https://www.pewresearch.org/short-reads/2019/01/17/where-millennials-end-and-generation-z-begins/.

Doherty-Sneddon, G., and F. G. Phelps. "Gaze Aversion: A Response to Cognitive or Social Difficulty?" *Memory & Cognition* 33, no. 4 (June 1, 2005): 727–33. https://doi.org/10.3758/ BF03195338.

Drinko, Clay. "We're Worse at Listening Than We Realize," *Psychology Today* (August 4, 2021), https://www.psychologytoday.com/us/blog/play-your-way-sane/ 202108/were-worse-listening-we-realize.

Edwards, Renee. "Listening and Message Interpretation." *International Journal of Listening* 25, no. 1–2 (January 31, 2011): 47–65.

https://doi.org/10.1080/10904018.2011.536471.

Emmanuel, Richard, Jim Adams, Kim Baker, E.K Daufin, Coke Ellington, Elizabeth Fitts, Jonathan HImsel, Linda Holladay, and David Okeowo. "How College Students Spend Their Time Communicating." *International Journal of Listening* 22 (February 11, 2023): 13–28. https://doi.org/10.1080/10904010701802-139.

Erickesen, Kirsten S. "Technology Impact On Listening Skills – Journal of Global Engagement and Transformation." *The Journal of Global Engagement and Transformation* 3, no. 1 (February 18, 2023). https://everypiecematters.com/jget/volume03-issue01/technology-impact-on-listening-skills.html.

Franceschi, Gioia De, and Tania Rinaldi Barkat. "Task-Induced Modulations of Neuronal Activity along the Auditory Pathway." *Cell Reports* 37, no. 11 (December 14, 2021). https://doi.org/10.1016/j.celrep.2021.110115.

Francis, Pope. *Fratelli Tutti: Encyclical on Fraternity and Social Friendship.* New London, CT: Twenty-Third Publications, 2020.

———. "LVI World Communications Day, 2022 - Listening with the Ear of the Heart | Francis." The Holy See, February 18, 2023. https://www.vatican.va/content/francesco/en/messages/communications/documents/20220124-messaggio-comunicazioni-sociali.html.

Fredman, Joelle. "75% of Gen Z Candidates Consider Company D&I Efforts When Deciding Whether to Apply." RippleMatch, September 29, 2022. https://ripplematch.com/insights/75-of-gen-z-candidates-consider-company-di-efforts-when-deciding-whether-to-apply/.

Gabrielson, Timothy A. "Obedience." In *Lexham Theological Wordbook*, edited by Douglas Mangum and others. Lexham Bible Reference Series. Bellingham, WA: Lexham Press, 2014.

Gallup Inc. "U.S. LGBT Identification Steady at 7.2%." Gallup.com, Feb-

ruary 22, 2023. https://news.gallup.com/poll/470708/lgbt-identifica-
tion-steady.aspx.

Goman, Carol Kinsey. "Body Language of Listeners." *Global Listening
Centre* (blog), November 17, 2015. https://www.globallisteningcen-
tre.org/body-language-of-listeners/.

Gray, Peter. "Declining Student Resilience: A Serious Problem for Colleges." Psychology Today, September 22, 2023. https://www.psycholo-
gytoday.com/us/blog/freedom-learn/201509/declining-student-re-
silience-serious-problem-colleges.

Haroutunian-Gordon, Sophie. "Plato's Philosophy of Listening." *Educational Theory* 61, no. 2 (2011): 125–39. https://doi.org/10.1111/j.1741-
5446.2011.00395.x.

Hobson, Katherine. "Clicking: How Our Brains Are in Sync." Princeton
Alumni Weekly, March 30, 2018. https://paw.princeton.edu/arti-
cle/clicking-how-our-brains-are-sync.

HRDQ-U. "12 Barriers To Effective Listening & How To Overcome
Them." *HRDQ-U - Ideas for Learning* (blog), March 21, 2019.
https://hrdqu.com/communication-skills-training/learning-to-over-
come-barriers-to-listening-skills-in-the-workplace/.

Humphrey, Jake, and Damian Hughes. "Kieran Trippier: How Struggle
Made Me Stronger," n.d. https://www.thehighperformancepod-
cast.com/podcast/kierantrippier.

John Paul II, Pope St. *Crossing the Threshold of Hope.* Edited by Vittorio
Messori. Translated by Jenny McPhee and Martha McPhee. New York:
Alfred A. Knopf, 1994.

Jones, Susanne M. "Supportive Listening." *International Journal of Listening* 25, no. 1–2 (January 31, 2011): 85–103. https://doi.org/
10.1080/10904018.2011.536475.

Katz, Roberta, Sarah Ogilvie, Jane Shaw, and Linda Woodhead. *Gen Z,
Explained: The Art of Living in a Digital Age.* Chicago, IL: University

of Chicago Press, 2022. https://press.uchicago.edu/ucp/books/book/chicago/G/bo115838546.html.

Kavandi, Elham. "To Prompt It: How Does Self-Confidence Affect Listening Skill?" *International Journal of Innovation and Research in Educational Sciences* 9, no. 1 (2022).

Kawamichi, Hiroaki, Kazufumi Yoshihara, Akihiro T. Sasaki, Sho K. Sugawara, Hiroki C. Tanabe, Ryoji Shinohara, Yuka Sugisawa, et al. "Perceiving Active Listening Activates the Reward System and Improves the Impression of Relevant Experiences." *Social Neuroscience* 10, no. 1 (January 2, 2015): 16–26. https://doi.org/10.1080/17470919.2014.954732.

Kluger, Avraham N., and Guy Itzchakov. "The Power of Listening at Work." *Annual Review of Organizational Psychology and Organizational Behavior* 9, no. 1 (2022): 121–46. https://doi.org/10.1146/annurev-orgpsych-012420-091013.

Koester, Craig R. *Hebrews: A New Translation with Introduction and Commentary*. Vol. 36. Anchor Yale Bible. New Haven; London: Yale University Press, 2008.

Kohut, Heinz, and Charles B. Strozier. *Self Psychology and the Humanities: Reflections on a New Psychoanalytic Approach*. New York: W.W. Norton, 1985.

Korby, Holly. "Young Adults Are Struggling with Their Mental Health. Is More Childhood Independence the Answer?" KQED, December 20, 2022. https://www.kqed.org/mindshift/60624/young-adults-are-struggling-with-their-mental-health-is-more-childhood-independence-the-answer.

Korkmaz, Selma, and Ahmet Güneyli. "Impact of Technology-Assisted Context-Based Teaching on the Listening Skills of Teacher Candidates." *Eurasia Journal of Mathematics, Science and Technology Education* 13, no. 8 (July 28, 2017): 4669–77. https://doi.org/10.12973/

eurasia.2017.00957a.

Korn Ferry. "The Science of Listening," Q1, 2013. https://www.korn-ferry.com/insights/briefings-magazine/issue-13/514-the-science-of-listening.

Kutlák, Jiří. "Individualism and Self-Reliance of Generations Y and Z and Their Impact on Working Environment: An Empirical Study across 5 European Countries." *Problems and Perspectives in Management* 19, no. 1 (January 21, 2021): 39–52. https://doi.org/10.21511/ppm.19(1).2021.04.

Kveraga, Kestutis, Avniel S. Ghuman, and Moshe Bar. "Top-down Predictions in the Cognitive Brain." *Brain and Cognition* 65, no. 2 (November 2007): 145–68. https://doi.org/10.1016/j.bandc.2007.06.007.

Leonard, Victoria, and Elizabeth Coleman. "Listening." In *Interpersonal Communication : Context and Connection.* Academic Senate for California Community Colleges Open Educational Resources Initiative, 2022. https://socialsci.libretexts.org/Bookshelves/Communication/Interpersonal_Communication/Interpersonal_Communication%3A_Context_and_Connection_(OERI)/06%3A_Listening/6.05%3A_Barriers_to_Listening.

Lev-Ari, Shiri. "Comprehending Non-Native Speakers: Theory and Evidence for Adjustment in Manner of Processing." *Frontiers in Psychology* 5 (2015).

Lindahl, Kay. "The Sacred Art of Listening." The Listening Center, February 18, 2023. http://www.sacredlistening.com/tlc_listening101.htm.

Lozano, Neal. *Unbound: A Practical Guide to Deliverance.* Grand Rapids, MI: Chosen, 2010.

Lukianoff, Greg, and Jonathan Haidt. *The Coddling of the American Mind: How Good Intentions and Bad Ideas Are Setting Up a Generation for Failure.* New York: Penguin Books, 2018.

Maloni, Michael, Mark S. Hiatt, and Stacy Campbell. "Understanding the

Work Values of Gen Z Business Students." *The International Journal of Management Education* 17, no. 3 (November 1, 2019): 100320. https://doi.org/10.1016/j.ijme.2019.100320.

Merriam-Webster. "Dictionary by Merriam-Webster." In *Merriam-Webster*, February 18, 2023. https://www.merriam-webster.com/.

Michelson, Tzvi, and Avraham Kluger. "Can Listening Hurt You? A Meta-Analysis of the Effects of Exposure to Trauma on Listener's Stress." *International Journal of Listening* 37, no. 1 (January 2, 2023): 1–11. https://doi.org/10.1080/10904018.2021.1927734.

Miller, William, and Stephen Rollnick. *Motivational Interviewing: Helping People Change.* 3rd ed. New York: The Guilford Press, 2012.

Minehart, Rebecca D., Benjamin B. Symon, and Laura K. Rock. "What's Your Listening Style?" *Harvard Business Review*, May 31, 2022. https://hbr.org/2022/05/whats-your-listening-style.

Minson, Julia A., and Charles A. Dorison. "Why Is Exposure to Opposing Views Aversive? Reconciling Three Theoretical Perspectives." *Current Opinion in Psychology* 47 (October 1, 2022): 101435. https://doi.org/10.1016/j.copsyc.2022.101435.

Mitchell, Travis. "On the Cusp of Adulthood and Facing an Uncertain Future: What We Know About Gen Z So Far." *Pew Research Center's Social & Demographic Trends Project* (blog), May 14, 2020. https://www.pewresearch.org/social-trends/2020/05/14/on-the-cusp-of-adulthood-and-facing-an-uncertain-future-what-we-know-about-gen-z-so-far-2/.

Monster Inc. "What Workforce Diversity Means for Gen Z." Monster, May 20, 2023. https://hiring.monster.com/resources/workforce-management/diversity-in-the-workplace/workforce-diversity-for-millennials/.

Moore, Catherine. "What Is The Negativity Bias and How Can It Be Overcome?" Positive Psychology, December 30, 2019. https://positivepsychology.com/3-steps-negativity-bias/.

Mukamel, Roy, Arne D. Ekstrom, Jonas Kaplan, Marco Iacoboni, and Itzhak Fried. "Single Neuron Responses in Humans during Execution and Observation of Actions." Current Biology : CB 20, no. 8 (April 27, 2010): 750–56. https://doi.org/10.1016/j.cub.2010.02.045.

Murphy, Kate. You're Not Listening: What You're Missing and Why It Matters. New York, NY: Celadon Books, 2021.

Murthy, Vivek. "Our Epidemic of Loneliness and Isolation: The U.S. Surgeon General's Advisory on the Healing Effects of Social Connection and Community," May 2, 2023. https://www.hhs.gov/sites/default/files/surgeon-general-social-connection-advisory.pdf.

Murthy, Vivek. "Protecting Youth Mental Health The U.S. Surgeon General's Advisory," 2021. https://www.ncbi.nlm.nih.gov/books/NBK-575984/pdf/Bookshelf_NBK575984.pdf.

Nichols, Ashley Orme. "Listening Types." In Making Conflicts Suck Less: The Basics. Boise State University eCampus, 2020. https://open.maricopa.edu/makingconflictsuckless/chapter/listening-types/.

Nouwen, Henri J. M. Bread for the Journey: A Daybook of Wisdom and Faith. 1st ed. San Francisco: Harper SanFrancisco, 1997.

Office of the Surgeon General. "Social Media and Youth Mental Health — Current Priorities of the U.S. Surgeon General," June 21, 2023. https://www.hhs.gov/surgeongeneral/priorities/youth-mental-health/social-media/index.html.

Orme Nichols, Ashley. "Barriers to Effective Listening." In Making Conflicts Suck Less: The Basics. Pressbooks, 2020. https://open.maricopa.edu/makingconflictsuckless/chapter/barriers-to-effective-listening/.

Owen Hargie. Skilled Interpersonal Communication: Research, Theory and Practice, 5th Ed. 5th ed. New York: Routledge, n.d.

"Parents Now Spend Twice as Much Time with Their Children as 50 Years Ago," *The Economist.* February 18, 2023. https://www.economist.com/graphic-detail/2017/11/27/parents-now-spend-twice-as-much-time-with-their-children-as-50-years-ago.

Pellegrino, G. di, L. Fadiga, L. Fogassi, V. Gallese, and G. Rizzolatti. "Understanding Motor Events: A Neurophysiological Study." *Experimental Brain Research* 91, no. 1 (1992): 176–80. https://doi.org/10.1007/BF00230027.

Pérez-González, David, Manuel S. Malmierca, and Ellen Covey. "Novelty Detector Neurons in the Mammalian Auditory Midbrain." *The European Journal of Neuroscience* 22, no. 11 (December 2005): 2879–85. https://doi.org/10.1111/j.1460-9568.2005.04472.x.

"Peter Bull - Psychology, University of York." Accessed July 19, 2023. https://www.york.ac.uk/psychology/staff/honoraryandassociates/peb1/.

Peterson, Sarah. "Secondary Traumatic Stress." The National Child Traumatic Stress Network, January 30, 2018. https://www.nctsn.org/trauma-informed-care/secondary-traumatic-stress.

Plato, and C. D. C. Reeve. *A Plato Reader: Eight Essential Dialogues.* Indianapolis, IN: Hackett, 2012.

Pugle, Michelle. "Helping vs. Enabling: What's the Difference?" Psych Central, March 14, 2018. https://psychcentral.com/health/what-is-the-difference-between-supporting-and-enabling.

Radesky, Jenny S., Caroline J. Kistin, Barry Zuckerman, Katie Nitzberg, Jamie Gross, Margot Kaplan-Sanoff, Marilyn Augustyn, and Michael Silverstein. "Patterns of Mobile Device Use by Caregivers and Children During Meals in Fast Food Restaurants." *Pediatrics* 133, no. 4 (April 1, 2014): e843–49. https://doi.org/10.1542/peds.2013-3703.

Remembering Mr. Rogers (1994/1997), 2016. https://www.youtube.com/watch?v=djoyd46TVVc.

Ripplematch. "Diversity in the Workplace: 2022-2023 Insight Report," May 20, 2023. https://resources.ripplematch.com/2022-2023-diversity-in-the-workplace.

Rogers, Carl R. "Empathic: An Unappreciated Way of Being." *The Counseling Psychologist* 5, no. 2 (June 1975): 2–10. https://doi.org/10.1177/001100007500500202.

Rogers, Carl R, and Richard E Farson. "Active Listening." In *Communicating in Business Today*. D.C Heath and Company, 1987. https://wholebeinginstitute.com/wp-content/uploads/Rogers_Farson_Active-Listening.pdf.

Savitsky, Kenneth, Boaz Keysar, Nicholas Epley, Travis Carter, and Ashley Swanson. "The Closeness-Communication Bias: Increased Egocentrism among Friends versus Strangers." *Journal of Experimental Social Psychology* 47, no. 1 (January 2011): 269–73. https://doi.org/10.1016/j.jesp.2010.09.005.

Saylor Academy. "CUST104: Boundless Communications: 'Causes of Poor Listening,'" February 17, 2023. https://learn.saylor.org/mod/page/view.php?id=18743.

Schurz, Matthias, Joaquim Radua, Matthias G. Tholen, Lara Maliske, Daniel S. Margulies, Rogier B. Mars, Jerome Sallet, and Philipp Kanske. "Toward a Hierarchical Model of Social Cognition: A Neuroimaging Meta-Analysis and Integrative Review of Empathy and Theory of Mind." *Psychological Bulletin* 147, no. 3 (March 2021): 293–327. https://doi.org/10.1037/bul0000303.

Second Vatican Council. "Gaudium et Spes: Pastoral Constitution on the Church in the Modern World," n.d. https://www.vatican.va/archive/hist_councils/ii_vatican_council/documents/vat-ii_const_19651207_gaudium-et-spes_en.html.

"Secondary Traumatic Stress," April 25, 2023. https://www.acf.hhs.gov/trauma-toolkit/secondary-traumatic-stress.

Segal, Elizabeth, Karen Gerdes, Cynthia Leitz, M. Alex Wagaman, and Jennifer Geiger. *Assessing Empathy*, 2023. http://cup.columbia.edu/book/assessing-empathy/9780231543880.

Sherlock, Mary, and Danielle L. Wagstaff. "Exploring the Relationship between Frequency of Instagram Use, Exposure to Idealized Images, and Psychological Well-Being in Women." *Psychology of Popular Media Culture* 8, no. 4 (2019): 482–90. https://doi.org/10.1037/ppm0000182.

Silen, W., T. E. Machen, and J. G. Forte. "Acid-Base Balance in Amphibian Gastric Mucosa." *The American Journal of Physiology* 229, no. 3 (September 1975): 721–30. https://doi.org/10.1152/ajplegacy.1975.229.3.721.

SJ, William F. Lynch. *Images of Hope: Imagination as Healer of the Hopeless*. University of Notre Dame Pess, 1974.

Snow, David P. "Gesture and Intonation Are 'Sister Systems' of Infant Communication: Evidence from Regression Patterns of Language Development." *Language Sciences (Oxford, England)* 59 (January 2017): 180–91. https://doi.org/10.1016/j.langsci.2016.10.005.

Spunt, Robert P. "Mirroring, Mentalizing, and the Social Neuroscience of Listening." *International Journal of Listening* 27, no. 2 (May 1, 2013): 61–72. https://doi.org/10.1080/10904018.2012.756331.

St. Augustine. *The Confessions*, 2023. https://www.alibris.com/search/books/isbn/9781565480841.

Staffing Industry Analysts. "75% of Gen Z to Reconsider Applying at a Company with Unsatisfactory D&I Efforts." Staffing Industry, September 19, 2022. https://www2.staffingindustry.com/Editorial/Daily-News/75-of-Gen-Z-to-reconsider-applying-at-a-company-with-unsatisfactory-D-I-efforts-63021.

Stickley, Theodore. "From SOLER to SURETY for Effective Non-Verbal Communication." *Nurse Education in Practice* 11, no. 6 (November

2011): 395–98. https://doi.org/10.1016/j.nepr.2011.03.021.

Storch, Sharon L., and Anna V. Ortiz Juarez-Paz. "Family Communication: Exploring the Dynamics of Listening with Mobile Devices." *International Journal of Listening* 32, no. 2 (May 4, 2018): 115–26. https://doi.org/10.1080/10904018.2017.1330657.

Stoy Corps. "Great Questions," February 18, 2023. https://storycorps.org/participate/great-questions/.

Sundaram, D.S., and Cynthia Webster. "The Role of Nonverbal Communication in Service Encounters." *Journal of Services Marketing* 14, no. 5 (January 1, 2000): 378–91. https://doi.org/10.1108/0887604001034-1008.

Tang, C., L. S. Hamilton, and E. F. Chang. "Intonational Speech Prosody Encoding in the Human Auditory Cortex." *Science* 357, no. 6353 (August 25, 2017): 797–801. https://doi.org/10.1126/science.aam8577.

Technologies, AVG. "The AVG 2015 Digital Diaries Executive Summary," January 1, 2015.

The Beauty of Listening. Taize, France, 2011. https://www.youtube.com/watch?v=u7MhqIe_zC0.

The Survey Center on American Life. "Generation Z and the Future of Faith in America," 2022. https://www.americansurveycenter.org/research/generation-z-future-of-faith/.

Thompson, Bob Sullivan and Hugh. "Now Hear This! Most People Stink at Listening [Excerpt]." Scientific American, May 20, 2023. https://www.scientificamerican.com/article/plateau-effect-digital-gadget-distraction-attention/.

Thompson, Curt. *The Soul of Shame: Retelling the Stories We Believe about Ourselves.* Downers Grove, Illinois: InterVarsity Press, 2015.

Timsit, Annabelle. "Smartphones Are Disrupting the Crucial Connections between Parents and Their Babies." Quartz, July 31, 2019. https://qz.com/1674835/technology-is-interfering-with-the-parent-child-relationship/.

Tun, Patricia A., Sandra McCoy, and Arthur Wingfield. "Aging, Hearing Acuity, and the Attentional Costs of Effortful Listening." *Psychology and Aging* 24, no. 3 (September 2009): 761–66. https://doi.org/ 10.1037/a0014802.

UN Secretary General. "International Youth Year: Participation, Development, Peace." Report of the Secretary General. United Nations, June 1981.   https://digitallibrary.un.org/record/21539/files/A_36_215-EN.pdf.

Underwood, Kacey. "Yampa Valley Sustainability Council - Annual Report 2021." *YVSC* (blog), May 20, 2023. https://yvsc.org/annual-reports/.

University of Minnesota Libraries. *Communication in the Real World: An Introduction to Communication Studies, Chapter 5.2 - Barriers to Effective Listening.* Publisher: University of Minnesota Libraries Publishing edition, 2016., 2016. https://open.lib.umn.edu/communication/chapter/5-2-barriers-to-effective-listening/.

University of Permian Basin. "How Much of Communication Is Nonverbal? | UT Permian Basin Online," May 20, 2023. https://online.utpb.edu/about-us/articles/communication/how-much-of-communication-is-nonverbal/.

Wang, Yanqing, and Hong Chen. "Are Human Resource Managers with Good Listening Competency More Likely to Avoid Job Burnout?" *BMC Public Health* 22, no. 1 (February 7, 2022): 246. https://doi.org/10.1186/s12889-022-12618-x.

Washington University School of Law. "The Socratic Method: Why It's Important to the Study of Law," May 29, 2013. https://onlinelaw. wustl.edu/blog/the-socratic-method-why-its-important-to-the-study-of-law/.

Watzlawick, Paul, and Janet Beavin. "Some Formal Aspects of Communication." *American Behavioral Scientist* 10, no. 8 (June 26, 2023). https://doi.org/10.1177/0002764201000802.

What Is Mentionable Is Manageable: Mister Rogers, 2023. https://www.pbslearningmedia.org/resource/mentionable-manageable-mister-rogers-video/meet-the-helpers/.

William Roper. "The Life of Sir Thomas More." Fordham University, 1556.

Wolvin, Andrew D. *Listening*. Madison: Brown & Benchmark, 1996.

———. "Listening, Understanding, and Misunderstanding." In *21st Century Communication: A Reference Handbook*, by William Eadie, 137–46. 2455 Teller Road, Thousand Oaks California 91320 United States: SAGE Publications, Inc., 2009. https://doi.org/10.4135/9781412964-005.n16.

Worley, Peter. "Open Thinking, Closed Questioning: Two Kinds of Open and Closed Question." *Journal of Philosophy in Schools* 2, no. 2 (November 29, 2015). https://doi.org/10.21913/JPS.v2i2.1269.

Yao, Pan-tong, Jia Shen, Liang Chen, Shaoyu Ge, and Qiaojie Xiong. "Cortical Ensemble Activity Discriminates Auditory Attentional States." *Molecular Brain* 12, no. 1 (October 17, 2019): 80. https://doi.org/10.1186/s13041-019-0502-z.

"Youth | UNESCO." Accessed July 19, 2023. https://www.unesco.org/en/youth.

Zenger, Jack, and Joseph Folkman. "What Great Listeners Actually Do." *Harvard Business Review*, July 14, 2016. https://hbr.org/2016/07/what-great-listeners-actually-do.

Made in the USA
Monee, IL
04 November 2023